Culture and Teaching

REFLECTIVE TEACHING
AND THE SOCIAL CONDITIONS OF SCHOOLING
A Series for Prospective and Practicing Teachers
—Daniel P. Liston and Kenneth M. Zeichner, Series Editors—

❖ ❖ ❖

Zeichner/Liston • Reflective Teaching: An Introduction

Liston/Zeichner • Culture and Teaching

Culture and Teaching

Daniel P. Liston
University of Colorado, Boulder
Kenneth M. Zeichner
University of Wisconsin, Madison

LEA LAWRENCE ERLBAUM ASSOCIATES, PUBLISHERS
1996 Mahwah, New Jersey

Lawrence Erlbaum Associates, Inc., Publishers
10 Industrial Avenue
Mahwah, New Jersey 07430

Cover design by Gail Silverman
Cover art by Danny Silverman

Library of Congress Cataloging-in-Publication Data

Liston, Daniel Patrick
    Culture and teaching / Daniel P. Liston, Kenneth M.
Zeichner.
        p.   cm.
    Includes bibliographical references (p.   ) and index.
    ISBN 0-8058-8051-8 (pbk. : alk. paper)
    1. Education—Social aspects—United States—Case
studies.   2. Teaching—Social aspects—United
States—Case studies.   3. Multicultural education—United States—Case studies.   4. Home and
school—United States—Case studies.   5. Critical pedagogy—United States.   I. Zeichner, Kenneth M.   II.
Title.
LC191.4.L567 1996
370.19'2—dc20   96-18080
                                                      CIP

Printed in the United States of America
10 9 8 7 6 5 4 3 2 1

This book is dedicated to our children:
Ira and Matthew Liston
and Aaron, Jordon, and Noah Zeichner

CONTENTS

II. PUBLIC ARGUMENTS   55

III. A FINAL ARGUMENT, AND SOME SUGGESTIONS AND RESOURCES FOR FURTHER REFLECTION   83

SERIES PREFACE

AN ESSENTIAL SERIES INTRODUCTION

Whereas many readers rarely read introductory material, we hope you will continue. The success of this book depends, in large part, on how you use it. In what follows we outline some of our key assumptions and we suggest ways for approaching the material in each book of this series entitled, "Reflective Teaching and the Social Conditions of School." First we identify some of our reasons for creating this series. We then relate a bit about our dissatisfaction with how teacher education is usually conducted and how it can be changed. Finally we outline suggestions for ways to best utilize the material in this and subsequent texts.

About 4 years ago we were asked to develop further the ideas outlined in our book *Teacher Education and the Social Conditions of Schooling* (Liston & Zeichner, 1991). It was suggested that we take our basic approach to teacher reflection and our ideas about teacher education curricula and put them into practice. The proposal was attractive and the subsequent endeavor proved to be very challenging. It never seems easy to translate educational "shoulds" and possibilities into schooling "cans" and realities. But we think (and we hope) we have made progress in that effort by designing a series of books intended to help prospective, beginning, and experienced teachers to reflect on their profession, their teaching, and their experiences. We are pleased and delighted to have the opportunity to share this work with you. We hope you will find these texts to be engaging and useful.

We are two university teacher educators, both former elementary teachers, who have worked in inner-city, small town, and suburban elementary and middle schools. We are committed to public schools as democratic institutions, as places of learning in which people of all walks of life come to learn how to live together in a democratic society. Although we are personally committed to ways of working and living together that are much more collaborative than exist today—we are educators first, realists second, and dreamers third. It is our firm belief that an education that engages prospective and practicing teachers' heads and hearts, their beliefs and passions, needs to be fair and honest. We have not written these texts to convince you to see schools and society as we do but rather to engage you in a consideration of crucial issues that all teachers need to address. Once engaged we hope that you will be better able to articulate your views, responses, and responsibilities to students and parents, and come to better understand aspects of your role as a teacher in a democratic society.

IMPACTS OF THE SOCIAL CONDITIONS
OF SCHOOLING

Prospective teachers need to be prepared for the problems and challenges of public schooling. All too often the focus in schools (departments and colleges) of education remains strictly on the processes that occur within the classroom door and inside the school walls. Many teacher education programs tend to emphasize instructional methodology and the psychology of the learner in the university course work and to underscore survival strategies during student teaching. These are certainly important elements in any teacher's preparation and ones that cannot be ignored. But classrooms and schools are not insulated environments. What goes on inside schools is greatly influenced by what occurs outside of schools. The students who attend and the teachers and administrators who work within those walls bring into the school building all sorts of cultural assumptions, social influences, and contextual dynamics. Unless some concerted attention is given to those assumptions, influences, and dynamics, to the reality of school life and to the social conditions of schooling, our future teachers will be ill prepared.

We are living in a time of remarkable change, a time of social and political transformation. In an era that promises to be rife with social controversies and political difficulties, in which public schooling will increasingly come under attack, during which we will see marked changes in this country's cultural demographic make-up, in which there will be great pressure to transform public schools into private-for-profit enterprises, our teaching workforce must be well prepared. Future teachers cannot, on their own, solve the many societal issues confronting the schools, but they should certainly know what those issues are, have a sense of their own beliefs about those issues, and understand the many ways in which those issues will come alive within their school's walls. Poverty and wealth, our culture of consumerism, what seems to be an increasing amount of violent behavior, and the work pressures of modern life affect the children who attend our public schools. Public attitudes about competition and excellence, race and ethnicity, gender roles and homosexuality, and the environment affect students inside and outside of schools. One can be certain that the issues that affect all of our lives outside of schools will certainly influence students inside their schools.

EXAMINING THE SOCIAL CONDITIONS
OF SCHOOLING

Probably the best way to begin to examine contextual issues such as these is to be "watchful" early on in one's professional preparation, to experience features of the social conditions of schooling, and then to examine the experience and what we know about the social and cultural context of schooling. We encourage prospective and practicing teachers to do this. But teacher preparation programs often are not organized in a fashion that would encourage the discussion and examination of these sorts of shared experiences. What traditionally are called *social foundations* courses are typically not school-based, but set apart from some of the more realistic, practical, and engaged dilemmas of schooling. In schools of education we frequently teach what the sociology or philosophy of education has to say about schools but we tend to teach it as sociologists or philosophers, not as teachers struggling with crucial and highly controversial issues. Thus, in our own work with prospective and practicing teachers we have developed ways to examine contextual issues of schooling and to enable ourselves and students to articulate our ideas, beliefs, theories, and feelings about those issues. The books in this series attempt to utilize some of these insights and to pass along to others the content and the processes we have found useful.

When students and faculty engage in discussions of the social and political conditions of schooling and the effects of these conditions on students and schools, it is likely that the talk will be lively and controversies will emerge. In this arena there are no absolutely "right" or "wrong" answers. There are choices, frequently difficult ones, choices that require considerable discussion, deliberation, and justification. In order for these discussions to occur we need to create classroom settings that are conducive to conversations about difficult and controversial issues. The best format for such discussion is not the debate, the (in)formal argument, or dispassionate and aloof analysis. Instead the most conducive environment is a classroom designed to create dialogue and conversation among participants with differing points of view. There isn't a recipe or formula that will ensure this type of environment but we think the following suggestions are worth considering.

It is important for individuals using these texts to engage in discussions that are sensitive and respectful toward others, and at the same time challenge each other's views. This is not an easy task. It requires each participant to come to the class sessions prepared, to listen attentively to other people's views, and to address one another with a tone and attitude of respect. This means that when disagreements between individuals occur, and they inevitably will occur, each participant should find a way to express that disagreement without diminishing or attacking the other individual. Participants in these professional discussions need to be able to voice their views freely and to be sensitive toward others. Frequently, this is difficult to do. In discussions of controversial issues, ones that strike emotional chords, we are prone to argue in a way that belittles or disregards another person and their point of view. At times, we try to dismiss both the claim and the person. But if the discussions that these books help to initiate are carried on in that demeaning fashion, the potential power of these works will not be realized. A discussion of this paragraph should occur before discussing the substance raised by this particular text. It is our conviction that when a class keeps both substance and pedagogy in the forefront it has a way of engaging individuals in a much more positive manner. From our own past experiences we have found that during the course of a class's use of this material it may be quite helpful to pause and focus on substantive and pedagogical issues in a conscious and forthright manner. Such time is generally well spent.

UNDERSTANDING AND EXAMINING PERSONAL BELIEFS ABOUT TEACHING AND SCHOOLING

It is also our belief that many educational issues engage and affect our heads and our hearts. Teaching is work that entails both thinking and feeling; those who can reflectively think and feel will find their work more rewarding and their efforts more successful. Good teachers find ways to listen to and integrate their passions, beliefs, and judgments. And so we encourage not only the type of group deliberation just outlined but also an approach to reading that is attentive to an individual's felt sense or what some might call "gut" level reactions. In the books in this series that contain case material and written reactions to that material, along with the public arguments that pertain to the issues raised, we believe it is essential that you, the reader, attend to your felt reactions, and attempt to sort out what those reactions tell you. At times it seems we can predict our reactions to the readings and discussions of this material while at other times it can invoke reactions and feelings that surprise us. Attending to those issues in a heartfelt manner, one that is honest and forthright, gives us a better sense of ourselves as teachers and our understandings of the world. Not only do students walk into schools with expectations and assumptions formed as a result of life experiences but so do their teachers. Practicing and prospective teachers can benefit from thinking about their expectations and assumptions. Hopefully, our work will facilitate this sort of reflection.

ABOUT THE BOOKS IN THIS SERIES

The first work in this series, *Reflective Teaching: An Introduction*, introduces the notion of teacher reflection and develops it in relation to the social conditions of schooling. Building on this concept, the second work in the series, *Culture and Teaching*, encourages a reflection on and examination of issues connected to teaching in a pluralistic society. Subsequent works will use a similar reflective approach to examine prominent educational issues and to explore further our understanding of teaching. Topics will include gender and teaching; stories, literacy, and teaching; bilingual students and mainstream teachers; and democracy and teaching. The structure of the works will vary depending on our various contributors, the content of the work, and the ways we can conceive of encouraging reflective practice. But each of the works will take as its central concern the reflective examination of our educational practice within larger social contexts and conditions.

SERIES ACKNOWLEDGMENTS

Two individuals have been essential to the conception and execution of this series. Kathleen Keller, our first editor at St. Martin's Press (where the series originated), initially suggested that we further develop the ideas outlined in *Teacher Education and the Social Conditions of Schooling* (Liston &

Zeichner, 1991). Kathleen was very helpful in the initial stages of this effort. Naomi Silverman, our current and beloved editor at Lawrence Erlbaum Associates, has patiently and skillfully prodded us along attending to both the "big picture" and the small details. We are thankful and indebted to both Kathleen and Naomi.

—Daniel P. Liston
—Kenneth M. Zeichner

Culture and Teaching

PREFACE

A work focused on culture and teaching will inevitably face expectations that it cannot meet and controversies that it cannot solve. If we begin with the simple assumptions that culture involves a set of meanings and meaning systems that people create and attach to their everyday lives and activities, and that teaching entails the facilitation and articulation of students' meaning systems, then we have before us a very large task indeed. Immediately questions arise: "Whose culture will be facilitated?" "Is there such a 'thing' as a common culture?" "What 'culture' does the student bring to the classroom?" and "What is the role of the teacher in this 'meaning-facilitation' process?". These and many more questions spring up. We do not presume to answer those questions in a definitive manner. Rather, and in keeping with this series on reflective teaching, we hope to engage you the reader in an exploration of these and other questions. We have designed this work in such a way that it will enable you to articulate your own "practical theories," your basic beliefs and assumptions, and to become acquainted with other points of view. If you come to this text with the expectation that we answer some central questions, you will probably be disappointed not only with this text and but also with the profession of teaching. We offer our view, but we do so not to assert the "truth." Instead, we hope to provide a medium for reaction and further interpretation. In the arena of culture and teaching, as in teaching in general, there are few simple and easy answers. We think that feature makes teaching challenging, engaging, enjoyable, and certainly frustrating.

The controversies that attend the topic of culture and teaching are many and quite intense. The questions just raised are not simply "academic" questions, but rather highlight and touch on issues that are highly personal, emotionally charged, and at times appear to be rather divided. Our own individual reactions to these issues are based in large part on our past experiences, our accumulated knowledge and understandings, and our core values. And as teachers, who we are as individuals affects both how and what we will teach and how we will view our students.

In the first volume of this series, *Reflective Teaching: An Introduction*, we explain that a central task in reflection entails an examination of our own theories and beliefs. These theories and beliefs, we argue, are formed and arise from our past experiences, our received knowledge, and our basic values. Part of reflective teaching entails an introspective and critical analysis of those experiences, understandings, and values. In arenas as controversial as the domain of culture and teaching, this sort of examination can be difficult. When we begin to uncover assumptions and beliefs that we want to support and ones that surprise us we need to be kind to ourselves and others. Reflection in this arena will necessarily take us on both an introspective journey and an examination of the social conditions of schooling. We need to know not only what we believe but what schools do. It has long been charged that our educational system privileges some and disenfranchises others. We believe that schools are not the equitable institutions that we would hope them to be. That seems to be a feature of schooling and one that deserves a great deal more attention. Hopefully this work will facilitate an examination of your own beliefs, acquaint you with the sentiments and arguments of others, and encourage you to look further into the social conditions of schooling. If these three goals are accomplished, our work will be a success.

CONTENT AND STRUCTURE

The structure of this work is fairly simple. It is organized in three basic parts. Part I includes three extended cases dealing with related aspects of culture and teaching, along with a range of preservice and practicing teachers', administrators', and parents' reactions to each case. Part II includes an elaboration of three "public arguments" pertaining to the issues raised in the cases in Part I. And Part III includes our own concluding statement about some of the issues raised throughout the work, activities for additional experiences and reflection, and a bibliography of additional resources.

The Case Studies

The three case studies in Part I focus on issues related to culture and teaching. In Case 1: "School and Home," we tell a story about a Euro-

American teacher who attempts to walk between an Hispanic student's life at school and situation at home. In Case 2: "Teachers and Cultural Identities," we describe an Anglo teacher's preparation for and her first year of teaching in a mixed ethnic setting. In Case 3: "Curriculum and Culture," we portray a school and a particular White teacher's efforts to examine issues related to a multicultural curriculum. These are not accounts of actual persons or particular schools, but rather composite narratives that combine a number of experiences and issues that teachers face today, and represent actual situations that teachers have experienced. We have chosen to underscore and explore the interactions between Anglo teachers and students of color because most public school teachers are Anglo and many students are not.

Each case study is followed by a set of reactions written by prospective and practicing teachers, parents, and administrators who we asked to read and respond to these stories. These represent some of the many and distinct ways people react to the issues presented in the case studies. A reading of these reactions not only informs us about the varied and multiple interpretations people make but also helps to articulate our own reactions. To facilitate this articulation we have tried to collect a broad spectrum of reactions. In the final section of Part I we offer three general reactions to the set of case studies collected here, in the form of three individuals' reactions to these case studies. Their responses seem to represent three distinct ways to interpret the material and they help to connect the particular issues presented in the case studies to the more general analyses outlined in the "public arguments" in Part II.

Between each case study and the reactions, and after the set of reactions for each case study, we have left space in the text for you to write your own reactions/reflections. People approach this task differently. Some find it easier to write their reactions after reading the case study; others find it helpful to wait until they have read others' reactions. We suggest jotting down your own reactions in both places. Reflection is neither a static nor unalterable process, but rather a dynamic affair. Hopefully, your reactions to the case material will change and develop over time. We want to encourage that process.

The Public Arguments

Whereas the power of case studies lies in their concrete rendering of particular problems and issues, the power of public argument comes from its ability to capture in a broader, more encompassing fashion, the individual experiences we encounter. In Part II we move from the particular realm of case studies to the more general arena of public arguments and present three very different views about culture and teaching. What we call *public arguments* or *public voices* are ways of tying together, in a somewhat coherent and sensible fashion, the distinct interpretations of the earlier case study material. We present *conservative, radical,* and *progressive* views of culture and teaching. We have used italics for these titles to indicate that they represent approximations of those views. Although William Bennett (1992) and Diane Ravitch (1991) might identify themselves as conservatives and Jane Roland Martin (1992) and Michael Apple (1993) would probably accept the label of radical, we doubt that any of these individuals would agree with all that we have included in their respective public arguments. It is also doubtful that either Nel Noddings (1992) or Ted Sizer (1992) would agree with all that we have included under the progressive label. Nevertheless, it is our sense that these three public arguments capture and express a synthesis of views that these and other similarly inclined authors have articulated. These renditions represent the kinds of claims that one reads in editorials, that guide policy formation, and that express individuals' general beliefs and values. In a work that attempts to connect what goes on inside and outside of schools it is essential that we examine the "public" articulation of what should go on inside of schools. For practicing and prospective teachers it is crucial that we not only learn how to discern the meaning and direction of these various voices but that we can identify and articulate our own reactions to these views.

At times, people feel that discussions about schooling have become much too political, that they harbor concerns that masquerade as educational while in reality are very little concerned with children and their learning. We tend to agree. Whereas many teachers see the classroom as the site for meaningful action, others seem to think of schools and the larger political arena as places where large egos can strut upon big and small stages. Again, we think there is some truth to this perception. But our belief is that when we draw too many sharp distinctions between what occurs inside and what happens outside the classroom, between the public worlds and our private worlds, we may be helping to create in our own perceptions unbridgeable gulfs between worlds that, in reality, are quite connected. It is our fear that if teachers ignore, demean, or belittle the "political" realm, then crucial public resources and funds will be more difficult to retain and we will miss the very real ways in which politics and power affect the children we educate. We certainly do not want to create an unreasonable set of expectations, or an enlarged list of so-called "public duties" for teachers, but we also cannot accept the view that the teacher's only and exclusive concern is with what occurs in the classroom. Whether we like it or not, what occurs within the classroom is dependent in so many ways on the larger contexts of our lives. The articulation of public arguments serves to highlight the distinct but general ways people come to view the issues associated with culture and teaching. The articulation of public arguments helps to identify more fully our own views and the views of others.

Our Own View

Finally, in Part III, we offer briefly our own reading of the issues associated with culture and teaching, and we outline a number of ways that both practicing and prospective teachers can engage in a further inquiry into these matters. We do not use this space as a place to develop fully our views on culture and teaching, but we do want to begin to elaborate our perspective—one that borrows elements from all three perspectives while maintaining a central allegiance to the radical or social reconstructionist orientation. Ours is one more view; we encourage you to develop your own. In this section, we provide a list of what we consider to be indispensable books and we outline some suggestions for teacher research and inquiry.

We did not create this book to provide a sense of immediate or ultimate resolution to the issues of culture, teaching, and schooling. We did create this text in the hopes that it would inform and provide further direction to those prospective and practicing teachers who want to examine difficult and controversial issues. These are difficult issues but issues that any competent teacher cannot ignore.

ACKNOWLEDGMENTS

A number of individuals have read parts of this work, have contributed to the reactions included in Part I, and/or have offered their comments and suggestions about the project. We have benefited from their comments and reactions and we acknowledge their contributions. Unfortunately, the creation of this text has taken a long time and so it is probably inevitable that we have left someone out. For that we apologize. The list is long and our indebtedness is great. However, we alone are responsible for the direction and substance of the text. We want to thank the following individuals: Julie Barbe, Tod Bartelson, Brigitte Boetigger, Matt Buchler, Angi Carey, Delia Da Cunha, Keesha Dair, Michael Dale, Amy Dawson, Jennifer Delille, Scott

Fletcher, Maggie Guntre, Zaretta Hammond, Heather Harris, Lise Inzzolino, David Kimmet, Cathy Lazarr, Cheryl Lehman, Meg Leimkuhler, Leanne Lockhart, Jen Martelli, Paul Michalec, Monteith Mitchell, Ofelia Miramontes, J. Noble, Kevin O'Dea, Diane Pazour, Lisa Perez, Nancy Pogsti, Stevi Quate, Sue Reid, Ben Rous, Phil Schnieder, Michele Seipp, Maria Timmons, Ingrid Unruh, Rex West, Fran Whitaker, Tim White, and John Zola. Landon Beyer, Martha M. Tevis, and Walter Ullrich read and commented on the entire text. As a result of their suggestions, the work improved. We also want to acknowledge the anonymous reviewers who offered helpful suggestions and criticisms during the early stages of conceptualizing the endeavor. Thank you.

—*Daniel P. Liston*
—*Kenneth M. Zeichner*

I

CASE STUDIES AND REACTIONS

What follows are three case studies, each one succeeded by a set of reactions. In each case study we have attempted to highlight distinct issues. We see this text as a springboard for classroom analyses and conversations, thus we do not initially spend a great deal of time elaborating the issues. We do, however, think it might be helpful to foreshadow some of the key issues, to alert you as to what to look out for. We hope this initial underscoring of the issues will enable you to read, react, discuss, and analyze further your understandings of this material. When we introduce the reactions, we highlight the thematic content of those reactions and later pose questions about some of the themes and issues. After each case study and each set of reactions we have left space for you to jot down your reactions to the material.

INTRODUCTION TO CASE 1

In "School and Home," the concepts of *cultural identity, cultural difference,* and *cultural bridges* are touched on. No matter what our race or ethnic background may be, we share with others certain norms, beliefs, and values. Individually, we are a part of larger cultural meaning systems and as a result of those meaning systems and our daily lived experiences we form and create a cultural identity. One person may be African American, Catholic, middle-class, and "entrepreneurially" oriented. Another individual may be

White, Baptist, working class, and rurally oriented. With each of those "cultural markers," with the experiences and lives lived, come beliefs and values that are shared with others. In "School and Home," Anna, Estella, and Estella's parents all have cultural identities. But these key players don't necessarily have similar cultural identities. Among these individuals there are cultural differences. At times we "automatically" assign certain values to particular cultural differences. For some northerners, an individual's southern accent is seen negatively. For some individuals, cultural differences are viewed as "out of the ordinary" and therefore amiss. In schools, cultural differences abound. If they are seen negatively the task of educating becomes very difficult. Frequently, educators have the task of communicating between and among individuals from distinct cultural backgrounds. They have to bridge cultural differences. In "School and Home" we see an attempt to bridge what Anna perceives as cultural differences.

CASE 1: "SCHOOL AND HOME"

Anna had been teaching for 3 years and she was beginning to feel more comfortable with the curriculum and her instructional style. She had worked at Pueblo Elementary School for all 3 years and felt like she knew her students. She was beginning to feel like she knew the community. Anna had always been intrigued by her students. Most of her 26 fifth graders were Hispanic. Some were recent immigrants from Mexico, whereas other families had lived in the area for three or four generations. Anna knew that she had been offered the position at Pueblo because she could speak some Spanish—but she never quite felt like she was truly bilingual. Anna was White, grew up on the East coast, and defined her own cultural identity around being Jewish. In many ways, her background was very different from her students but in some ways, the parallels were there and these intrigued her.

Anna's father, Steven, had grown up in a traditional Jewish household. His parents spoke Yiddish and he used to tell Anna of the joys and difficulties of being brought up as a Jew in a Gentile world. When he was at home he had to speak Yiddish but as he, his brother, and his sister grew older, they began to speak English in the home. His father forbid it and his mother didn't like it, but as time passed they worked out a compromise. At dinner, and in the living room and kitchen, the family spoke Yiddish. English could be spoken at other times and in other rooms. Anna's father loved to tell stories of when he was a young man and he always seemed to lace the tales with conflict and struggle, friendships, and accommodations. Growing up Jewish in a Gentile world never left her father. For Anna, these stories frequently conveyed a sense of the difficulty that seemed always to accompany efforts at personal accomplishments in a world where different cultures precariously coexisted.

So Anna was not new to the arena of cultural differences and her role as a White teacher in a predominantly Hispanic community brought with it challenges that reminded her of many of her father's stories. But as a teacher, Anna's slant on things was slightly different. Anna felt a great responsibility for helping all of her students learn. She sensed that all too often her students' accomplishments were much less than they could be. For 3 years Anna had been aware of the differences between her newly arrived Mexican children and the more established Hispanic community. At times, the newcomers would be taunted and picked on by the White and even other Hispanic children. Frequently, these students did not stay in her classroom for an entire year. Many of their parents were migrant farm workers and needed to move with the harvest season. This created a situation in which students left, in Anna's estimation, much too soon and too often. She frequently felt that she was just beginning to get a sense of one of her student's strengths and weaknesses, and then he or she would leave. Anna felt like she never got enough time with those kids and she wanted more.

But this year there was an exception. Estella Reyes had been with Anna last year in fourth grade and this year she was in her fifth-grade classroom. Estella's father was injured in a farm accident and so her family did not make its regular journey north. Early on, Anna had been impressed with Estella's quick wit and keen intelligence. But she saw those aspects of Estella mostly when she was with her friends. In class she performed adequately, almost perfunctorily. Estella had easily mastered English, in both its social and academic uses, and she was able to grasp almost intuitively the mathematical problems she was assigned. Estella worked quietly in the classroom, meeting the academic demands with ease but with little enthusiasm. Anna knew that Estella's academic ability could soon flower further or wither away. In the last 3 years, Anna had seen too many of her Hispanic girls lose interest in school and, in effect she thought, not adequately explore or expand their talents. This time Anna thought she would intervene. This time she was going to make sure that Estella and her family knew what the choices and options were. This time Anna wanted Estella and her family to make an informed choice about what she saw as Estella's future. She called Estella's house and asked her mother if she could stop by to talk. Estella's mother invited Anna to dinner for the next day. Anna had that evening to prepare.

First, Anna had to decide whether or not to write up her comments in Spanish so that she could be sure she expressed herself clearly. She had already decided not to ask her friend Peggy, who is truly bilingual, to come along to translate in the tough spots. Anna had decided that Peggy would be too much of a crutch in her interactions. She wanted to convey her own strengths and weaknesses to Estella's family and she hoped that her own efforts, no matter how stumbling, would put her on good terms with Estella's family. She decided to go it alone—without Peggy and without a written script. But her proficiency in Spanish wasn't the only potential problem that Anna was worried about. She knew that she would be entering another culture, one that tended to value differentially men's and women's roles. She wondered if her concerns would be seen as realistic. She thought that Estella's father might not listen. She feared that Estella's father would not want Estella to move outside of the traditional role for women. But Anna wanted to at least convey to Estella's mother and father her sense of Estella's intelligence and promise. She wanted Estella's abilities with language and math to be known and she wanted Estella's parents to know the options that Estella could have before her. Anna decided to rely on her stumbling ability with Spanish, her knowledge of the options available (but frequently closed) to girls like Estella, and her father's stories to get her through the evening.

The next evening Anna knocked on Estella's apartment door. Estella's family lived in a subsidized apartment complex, in one of the poorest sections of town. Estella's mother, Cecelia, quickly answered the door. Anna introduced herself and was invited into the apartment to sit at the kitchen table. Estella's father, Roberto, came to the table. He was still on crutches from the accident. Anna felt very uncomfortable at first. She spoke in halting Spanish while Cecelia and Roberto responded with a mixture of English and Spanish. But after awhile it seemed that the mixture of languages was conducive rather than a barrier to their conversation.

In her earlier telephone conversation Anna had said that she wanted to come to talk about Estella's talents. Cecelia and Roberto were eager to hear about their daughter's accomplishments. Anna related Estella's strengths in math and languages. She also told them about her own father's experiences with Yiddish and English, and how he used to tell her all sorts of stories when she was a young girl. Frequently, when Anna struggled to come up with a correct phrase or word, Estella would supply it for her. The evening and the dinner went along quickly and enjoyably but Anna hadn't yet posed the issue that had brought her to the table. After dinner Anna started to ask about some of the older girls who lived in the projects, girls that Anna had seen pass through the upper grades a few years earlier. Some of the girls were still in school, but many of them had children, and husbands or boyfriends. A few worked at the local fast food restaurants. Anna said that she thought that many of those girls' lives could have been different if they had stayed in school. She emphasized that Estella was a bright girl but that she feared that she might not be able to use and develop her talents fully if she did not receive the proper attention and support.

Anna talked about the middle and high school options the local district offered and she suggested that Estella should apply for the academically gifted option. Somehow Anna felt that the mood of the conversation changed at this point but she wasn't quite sure how it had changed. It did seem to her to take a more serious bent but she couldn't tell if the options she was laying out were being received as possibilities or if Estella's parents resented her attempted "intervention." Cecelia asked about the application procedures and while Anna and Cecelia talked Roberto got up from the table and went to the bedroom. After a bit more discussion Cecelia told Anna that she and Roberto would think about applying and if they decided to do so she could give Estella the application papers. They talked a bit more. Anna and Cecelia ended the evening with a discussion of the best way to roast peppers.

The next day Estella was absent. The following day she came to school. Anna was nervous and hesitant. She didn't know if she had approached the situation appropriately. Although she felt deep down inside that Estella deserved options in her life, Anna wasn't sure if she was the one to lay out those options. Anna wondered now if she should take the initiative to get the application forms or if she should wait for Estella to request them. She decided to wait a few days to see what would happen.

READER REACTIONS TO ANNA'S SITUATION

REACTIONS TO "SCHOOL AND HOME"

Anna's situation truly represents a conundrum. Possible reactions range from appraisals that what Anna did was very positive and commendable; that she misread and misunderstood the situation; to a view that such efforts are always a "balancing" act. Despite this range of reactions most individuals sense that what we have in Anna's case is a "problem" between two cultures—school and home. In such a setting the question of the teacher's role looms large. What should she or he do? How much responsibility should the teacher assume? Is it possible to "bridge" these two cultures? Do we have to confront the situation as a choice of "either school or home"? These are some of the questions and issues that arise.

A Commendable Action

Some individuals thought Anna did the right thing. They believed that as Estella's teacher, Anna needed to raise questions about Estella's future. Although they recognized that such an approach is fraught with problems, many people felt that Anna needed to "intervene."

> I think that Anna did the right thing by talking to Estella's parents about her academic future, attempting to show them a different direction for her. However, there's only so much she can do—she can't force them to do what she thinks they should do, which doesn't mean she should give up if nothing happens right away. Anna can let Estella know that she is there for her whenever she wants to move on the academic thing, but she shouldn't overdo it. She has to respect their culture. I think Anna can give Estella some information about what avenues would be available for her if she should change her mind later, or if parents change their mind and get enthusiastic.
>
> —Teacher

> This is a frustrating scenario. I think that Anna handled the situation appropriately by approaching Estella's parents. In fact, I think that it is the teacher's responsibility to open doors for the potential education of a student. Perhaps, Anna could approach Estella and ask her how she feels about the applications. Maybe the applications could even be sent to the home. However, I believe that if the family is not responsive to these actions, any further action would be an infringement and inappropriate. Anna must accept the decision made by Estella's parents. Both Anna and Estella's parents want the best for Estella. All Anna can do at this point is to provide the best possible education for Estella while she is in her classroom.
>
> —Student Teacher

A tough decision, even to bring up the issue. In the world today, where cultural values are either clung to, or rapidly metamorphosizing, it is hard to predict reactions to situations of cultural meeting. On the one hand, Anna's fears of Roberto's reactions were well-founded. ... On the other hand, and just as likely, Anna's fears were stereotypical by nature, not at all accounting for the possibility of Estella's parents being less traditional than others of their culture.

Anna's deferential demeanor when approaching the family was a nice approach. It would have been unwise to have taken an aggressive and determined stance. Anna may have an opinion of what she thinks is best for Estella as a bright woman; but Estella has also a distinct identity as a member of her culture, and the final decision is more influenced by her culture than her intellect. This would be difficult for any outsider (even with the best of intentions, as had Anna) to accept, but that acceptance would be crucial to Estella's sense of cultural self-esteem.

—Student Teacher

I do not think Anna overstepped her boundaries. I think she was brave to confront Estella's family and had only good intentions. After all, the family invited *her* to dinner. She didn't have to pound on their door for them to listen to her. And if Anna did not raise the issue, who would?

If Estella's parents disagree with Anna, at least Anna can tell herself that she tried and did what she thought was best for her student. If she had greatly offended Estella's family and culture, she would have received a more immediate, negative response at the dinner table.

I feel Anna did not use her white status in order to intimidate or be condescending with Anna's family. Then there would have been cultural conflict.

—Student Teacher

I think Anna's intervention was a very positive and appropriate way to be involved with one of her students. Her insight that Estella had great potential and a bright future, if she were to take the right course through continuing school, needed to be addressed to the parents. Anna could see that maybe education for women wasn't regarded as important as it should be in Estella's community, and this concerned Anna. Why not try, for Estella's sake, to enlighten the parents that their daughter could be so much more than so many older girls in town who were married, had boyfriends, and were working in fast food restaurants? Hopefully, Estella's parents would come to realize that their daughter's future could be so much more than all that.

—Prospective Teacher

A Potentially Offensive Intervention

Others thought Anna's actions were potentially offensive. These individuals felt that Anna may have unintentionally offended Estella and her parents. When one walks into another cultural setting it can be difficult to discern what is helpful and what is harmful. By presuming to "know" Estella's talents Anna may be treading on some rather thin ice. She may not understand the intricacies of Estella's culture or home life and she may be imposing some of her values on Estella and Estella's family.

> Anna may have offended Cecelia and Roberto by not getting to the point right away. By saying that Estella would not realize her potential if she didn't pursue schooling might sound like she is being biased toward career life. In my experience with Hispanics—many women feel extremely successful being a mother at an early age. It is a very family-oriented culture. Those girls who choose the family route may have done just that: chosen it.
> On the other hand, Estella's parents seemed receptive to her doing well in school. Maybe she should've said to Estella's parents, "I'm not sure what Estella wants to do in the future but here is an option because she excels in school. What are your feelings, Estella?" If Estella is excited by the idea (and if she doesn't seem apprehensive about her parents' reaction) then [Anna could] offer the papers—if Estella's parents don't seem offended. She should've asked Estella's parents how they specifically felt about what they would like to see her doing when she reached adulthood. I think she should try a more direct approach, starting with calling Estella's parents immediately and telling them she didn't want to offend them and she wants to know how they and Estella feel about Estella's future. She brought some cultural stereotypes into the meeting and maybe she [should] try to see Estella's family as Estella's family and not as a group of traveling migrant workers.
>
> —Prospective Teacher

> She has offended Estella's parents because she came out and said that Estella needed to change and be ready to be someone else after schooling. She pointed out that living in the projects and having a husband/boyfriend was a bad thing. Should she consider that perhaps Estella's parents don't want her to change? It's a hard situation because it seems that Estella needs to change. Her parents need to let her go. She needs to leave her past and culture behind in order to succeed. That is what Anna said to Estella's parents although she probably was not aware of it. In trying to help, she offended them. She brought up the touchy situation of racism and it was immediately changed to red peppers. Hearing about their daughter's talents alone did not cross this

line into racism. Anna made Estella's parents aware of their financial and social situation, in effect this gave them no hope in their present situation.

—Prospective Teacher

My gut feeling is that Anna approached this issue in the wrong way. First of all I don't think she should have relied on her Jewish background in order to establish a common ground and identity with the Hispanic way of life. I doubt that Cecelia and Roberto saw much similarity between Anna's life and their own and they probably resented being asked to view their life as no different than Anna's.

Also I think Anna made a mistake in approaching the family with the gifted program while assuming the role of friend. I think the family would have been much more receptive to the idea if Anna had written a "teacher" note to the parents and sent along the application information. The parents then would have been able to view Anna as a concerned teacher which [is a] role [that] would be culturally consistent with their own socialization. As it happened they had to hear the proposal from Anna in the role of "friend." A friend though is someone who can identify and understand and so Anna as a "friend" would be expected to understand the family's decision to not apply for the program, while Anna as a teacher had the right to encourage participation.

—Prospective Teacher

I can see Anna's point of view clearly and see that she had good intentions for Estella's success, but I think she assumed that she had more in common with the Reyes family than she actually did. First of all, once Mr. Reyes' leg healed, Estella would probably go back to skipping from town to town. Anna's suggestion that Estella could have a better life than the older girls in the community may have been offensive. Migrant workers have a defined culture and it's possible that the Reyes family began with Mrs. Reyes working at a fast food restaurant, then marrying Mr. Reyes. Anna is effectively saying that Estella's life will be wasted if she ends up like her parents. This puts the Reyes' on the defensive making them guilty if they are unable to support Estella's further education.

—Prospective Teacher

"She Needs to Assimilate"

For others Anna was, perhaps, not forceful enough. For these individuals, the central issue in this case is fairly clear: Estella needs to assimilate to the predominant values of American culture. Estella and her family live in the United States and if they are going to thrive here, they need to recognize the values and structure of this society. Not only do they need to recognize these values but Estella's parents need to help Estella embrace these values so that she can succeed.

I feel what Anna did (going to the parents' apartment) was the right thing. Speaking in Spanish, or at least trying to, also was a good thing. However, I believe she should have been more forceful with her proposal of getting Anna to advance. I realize that there are many traditional roles with the family, but I'm also sure they wouldn't mind too much that their daughter could succeed in life and stop having to be a migrant worker. After all, why did the parents come north of the border anyway? They came because there was greater opportunity in the U.S. than in Mexico. I'm sure they don't want their daughter ending up with a permanent fast food job. They want her to succeed. This is a big, big change for this family which I'm sure explains her absence from the class the day following her meeting. I do believe that the parents will relent as they want their daughter to proceed so that she can succeed. The father probably took some convincing, though the mother seemed like she wanted her daughter to continue this program without much hesitation. I am not sure whether Anna should have given the papers to Estella's parents the day Estella returned to class or if she should have waited. Going too fast might seem like Anna is rushing this; [by] the same token, if Anna waits too long to give the papers, the parents might decide to change their minds. I hope in the end Anna gave the papers to Estella and her parents, sooner rather than later, and that Estella is on her way to further her education.

—Prospective Teacher

Obviously, this is a tough situation. On the one hand, Anna's goals are to see that the children she teaches go as far as they can scholastically. To a woman who probably views herself as "liberated," Anna was right to try and aid Estella's academic career. On the other hand, perhaps Anna was projecting too much of her own culture onto the situation. Unable to see why a girl can't progress as far as a boy in a machismo culture, Anna quite possibly stepped on some toes. This brings on the much larger questions of what Estella's family was doing in America. Were they simply trying to assimilate to this culture to become "Americans"? This, in turn, lends itself to the even more complex issue of multicultural education: Are we African Americans, Asian Americans, Mexican Americans, or Americans? Do we weaken the country by highlighting how diverse we are? Or is that celebrating the foundation of America—the "melting pot" ideology? Personally, I don't believe there is much opportunity (under our present system) for people who celebrate their own culture (assuming it isn't gung-ho American). Assuming (again) that Estella's family came here for advancement, they would expedite this advancement by "playing by the rules." Estella, since she is now in America and an American, would be happier trying to be a doctor or professor (especially since she has tasted success and praise) than by just becoming what her antiquated (in her view—or at best Anna's) culture wants her to be—stifled.

—Prospective Teacher

"They" (Anna et al.) Just Don't Get It

Other individuals thought that the gap between Anna and Estella and her family was much too wide to be bridged or connected in one evening. These individuals feel Anna needs to take more time and perhaps pursue other avenues for understanding the situation and then communicating her concerns. Cross-cultural communication can be fraught with unacknowledged assumptions and miscommunication can result. Anna needs to take more care to assure adequate understanding and communication. She needs to become bilingual and bicultural.

> One evening is inadequate to establish adequate rapport to broach the subject of teenage motherhood, early marriage, and menial employment. There's the underlying message that Anna doesn't want Estella to be like "them." "Them" may well be dearly loved family members or friends. Anna had Estella for an entire year, why didn't she begin [establishing] rapport with Estella's family during the first year? ... After 3 years in a predominantly Hispanic student composition it is Anna's obligation to become "truly bilingual" if she desires to best serve her students. Beyond bilingualism, Anna needs to develop her anthropological perspectives. This would support her desires to make things different [and] diminish her quandary about how to effect her ultimate goals for her individual students. The issue is larger than Anna and Estella. Anna needs to develop peer support and principal support to make significant changes.
>
> —Parent

> I suspect Estella's parents probably had a completely different scenario pictured for Estella's future and it would take more than an evening for them to adjust to this new possibility and evaluate it. If they can accept the idea of their daughter in a sense venturing into unknown territory, there may be logistical problems to work out as well. If they plan to travel with the crops, then they will have to arrange a boarding situation for Estella, which might be impossible.
>
> My feeling about Anna's situation is that, while I think she has good intentions, I don't know if she went about this quite the right way. First, it might have been better to have someone more familiar with Estella's family situation help her to present this to Estella's family, someone who was fluent in Spanish. At the least, she could have tried to gather some more information

about what Estella's family's plans were. It doesn't sound like she did much listening at this dinner. I think Anna has Estella's best interests in mind, but she doesn't seem tuned in to Estella's world. Her knowledge of her own father's experiences does not give her knowledge of Hispanic culture or migrant worker culture or the particular culture and attitudes of Estella's home.

—ESL Teacher

I'm concerned that Anna believes a teacher might be welcome in a student's home by either parent or student. I wonder if she is motivated primarily by Estella's talents and intelligence? What if Estella was "average"? Anna has seemed to take into account the language situation but has not adequately prepared herself for the cultural ones. By making the analogy that because of her upbringing as a bilingual, bicultural, sometimes discriminated group member, as [being] similar to Estella and her family—she erroneously compares apples to oranges —both fruits, but not the same. Her barrier it seems is less language, more culture. Bilingual Peggy, unless bicultural or at least culturally tuned in, probably wouldn't have helped. Good try on Anna's part but she may have sabotaged future relations. Is Anna saying that a culture of women/girls that has children is inferior? Can she talk with Estella as she is probably the most bicultural? What about Hispanic outreach or community liaison? What does she lose if she persists? Is it worth it?

—Middle School Teacher

It's a Balancing Act

Still others see no easy answer or resolution to the issues presented in this case study. For some, Anna's situation represents a moral dilemma, one for which it is difficult to discern an unassailably "right" action. They recognize Anna's good intentions but feel that in spite of these intentions her actions could have unintended consequences. Being watchful, attentive, and sensitive to the distinct cultural communities seems to be an essential bit of advice here. It's a balancing act.

This situation represents a serious moral dilemma: respect Estella's culture for what it is or intervene to encourage her to move out of her culture into another. The risks in both instances are great. By not intervening and showing respect for Estella's cultural background, Anna is enabling Estella to lead a life with limited options for females and is, by neglect, promoting repression. Because Estella will lack the "cultural capital" needed to be economically successful in America, Anna would be neglecting one ethical dimension of her profession—to create environments in which students can thrive and grow. However, intervention if successful could begin the creation of barriers which might separate Estella not only from her culture but also from her family.

Ethically, I think Anna did what she needed to do. With great respect, she voiced her concerns and presented options for Estella's future. Without being patronizing, she approached the family responsibly, particularly as she entered the conversation with her shaky Spanish. Clearly, she was not cruel or uncaring in her concerns.

Cultures do change, we need to keep [that] in mind. As different cultures meet often head on, the two (or more) are forced to reconfigure. I am not suggesting that America is the mythical melting pot I was raised to believe in. I do know, however, that our culture (or cultures) have changed since I was a little girl. In Anna's decision about what to do, she is being responsible noting the changeability of culture while still holding on to respect of the family and its beliefs that Estella comes from.

A little Freire (1974) might be good for Anna also. Perhaps if she could get the families as well as her young students to consider their positions in the American scene and take action to become an acknowledged force, Anna might be able to effect more change.

—High School Teacher and Mother

Anna's story is complex. She seems to be driven by the memory of her own education and the power of her father's stories. But has she missed the point of her father's stories? Anna's childhood was certainly different than most of the children in her school, yet—she made it. Anna went on to become a teacher. She not only learned to adapt to the Gentile world, she learned to adopt it as well. Yet, her attempts to help Estella have failed, or have they?

When Anna visited Estella's parents, told stories of her own [and her father's] childhood, and praised Estella for her abilities, all seemed to go well. When Anna crossed that imaginary line and prescribed "proper attention and support," the meeting changed. To want to see that "proper" support is given is to imply that "improper" support is currently the situation. Yet Anna had raved about Estella's talents. Whatever Estella's parents were doing, it seemed to be working. Perhaps Anna would have done better to pass on the praise and tell her own stories, without dictating "proper" directions.

Of course, we don't know how this story ends. Of all I read so far I feel most optimistic about Anna's story. Anna was sensitive to her own cultural experiences, where Linda [see p. 33] was not. Anna was acting to "save" a child, where Sally [see p. 18] was engaged in battles of curriculum. Anna's battle certainly seems more human!

In a way, Anna did the right thing. She should let it rest at that. Do not press the application issue. She told her stories, she expressed her opinions honestly. She should respect Estella's parents and have faith that she has planted the "seeds" of a plant that will bear fruit another day!

—Administrator

I think Anna should have discussed Estella's possibilities with Estella before visiting her parents. That way she would have an idea of how Estella's family viewed a woman who is successful versus [more] traditional roles. Or maybe they're worried about money for continued education. And what about Estella's hope for the future, and why doesn't she act enthusiastic about her talent in schoolwork? I think that Anna could have accomplished more at Estella's parents' house if she would have had more to go on from talking with Estella.

But now that the situation has developed, I think Anna should pursue finding out about Cecelia and Roberto's reactions to her proposition for Estella's future. I don't think she should wait around for a request for the application. Anna should find out what their reservations are and what their hopes for Estella's future are. I also think Anna should ask Estella how she thought it went and what she was thinking about the whole situation. I agree that someone needs to help Estella with her future if that is indeed what Estella would want.

—Prospective Teacher

Even with the best of intentions, interacting cross culturally will always leave room for misunderstandings. One cannot act for fear of saying or doing the wrong thing. But a healthy dose of self-consciousness is useful. Once trust is built and understanding gained, the small differences remain small. Initially, though, there must be a foundation to build on. Anna's intentions are good but she may have rushed in too quickly. Perhaps she should have sought advice from a member of the community, simply met the parents without pushing the issue, and eventually had a student who was already in the gifted program speak to Estella. The best avenue of introduction will vary with the community, so it is best to know the community before jumping in. Also, Anna perceives a kindred spirit to the Hispanic community because of her own Jewish heritage, yet the Mexican family will not necessarily see those parallels. The Mexican family also does not share Anna's perspective of seeing other girls drop out as necessarily negative. Anna may have rushed in but her desire to learn about others and her sincere concern will carry her through small misunderstandings. Her sensitivity to the subtle changes in behavior will help her to remedy any misunderstandings, as they occur.

—Experiential Educator

READER REACTIONS TO "SCHOOL AND HOME"

SUMMARY AND ADDITIONAL QUESTIONS

At times, these case studies may raise more questions than they resolve. In the arena of culture and schooling we certainly hear distinct voices. There are those who maintain that the dominant White culture alienates other cultures to the degree that our public education system harms and oppresses children of color. To repair this harm, schools need to focus and center on the child's and his or her culture's contributions. Others believe that we all have to live up to standards and expectations and that the ones in school are no more White and oppressive than any other standards and expectations. It is time, these individuals say, to get on with the business of educating. Others maintain that some sort of balance has to be achieved. Accordingly, they claim that a Hispanic or African-American child need not be put in a position where they have to choose between home or school—a more integrative option is available. Although the issues are many, we think that the following questions begin to focus further some of the salient dilemmas. Some of the questions that come to mind include:

1. What does it mean to be bicultural and how does this relate to being bilingual? In a multicultural society is it a teacher's responsibility to become bicultural or multicultural?
2. Is Anna denigrating employment in fast food restaurants when she offers a perspective on Estella's future? What *is* Anna's perspective?
3. Should Anna pursue the issue and procure the application papers?
4. How would you describe Anna's cultural identity?
5. Do you think it was appropriate for Anna to make the initial contact and make the subsequent home visit?

INTRODUCTION TO CASE 2

In today's discussions about public school curricula and distinct cultures, the concept of a multicultural curriculum inevitably surfaces. Although individuals use the concept in a variety of fashions, it tends to accompany criticisms of the extant curriculum and a call for curricula that honor and recognize a broader range of cultures and cultures represented by the students taught. In "Curriculum and Culture," the term *multicultural curriculum* does not appear, but the concerns that accompany its usage will arise. The idea that a curriculum and the knowledge it contains may represent or favor one group over another is a central issue in this terrain.

The belief that some curricula help advance the economic futures of particular already advantaged groups over others is another concern that surfaces. How all of this is voiced and enacted by teachers and parents is a daily feature of public schools. In "Curriculum and Culture," these and other issues come to the foreground.

CASE 2: "CURRICULUM AND CULTURE"

Sally woke up with an "oh my gosh, what do we do now?" feeling. Last night members of the high school staff had met with a group of parents to discuss their concerns about the school. About a month earlier the newspapers had reported that her school's math and verbal SAT scores were among the lowest in the area. Parents were upset and they wanted to talk with the staff about the low scores. The discussion had surprised Sally. During the meeting, parents raised questions not only about the causes for the low scores but also about what their children were learning and how they were being taught. It was a challenging and demanding exchange.

Sally was new to the school. It was her second year of teaching English (literature and composition) and her first at Rosa Parks High School (RPHS). Although she had been apprehensive about the meeting she was actually relieved to hear what the parents had to say. Rosa Parks High School was located in a "fringe" neighborhood of a large midwestern city. It was one of the few areas in that urban region whose population was, as the locals described it, "salt and pepper." It was an integrated community with both White and Black residents. Most people described it as a lower middle-class neighborhood. It sat on the edge of the city's boundaries but not far enough removed from the urban center to be called suburban. A number of the parents were single working mothers. When a household contained two parents, usually both were engaged in some sort of full- or part-time work outside the home.

Sally was glad that the parents had raised concerns about the school's curriculum and the staff's instruction. She thought that most of the school's textbooks were out of date and uninteresting. Still feeling like a novice in the classroom, Sally relied heavily on the schools' existing English curriculum materials. But her trips to the school's storeroom always left her feeling somewhat depressed. The storeroom was filled with tattered textbooks and workbooks that were published 15 to 20 years ago. Not only was much of the material dated but it also seemed to be repetitive, drill-oriented, and basically boring. Last night, the parents made similar comments about the school curriculum but the parents used a slightly different language and expressed a somewhat different set of concerns.

At the outset of the meeting, the principal, Joe Riley, noted that most of the teachers attending the meeting taught either in the humanities or social studies departments. Math and science faculty were noticeably absent. Given the skewed nature of faculty representation Joe Riley thought it best to focus on the part of the high school curriculum that emphasized verbal, rather than mathematical content and skills.

The parents were not unanimous in their appraisal of what was wrong and what should be done but it seemed, in general, that there were two distinct views about what should be done. One group of vocal African-American parents led the charge early on and indicated that they were not happy with the kind of education their children were getting, especially in a school named after such a prominent figure in the civil rights movement. They said their kids were being given a poor White man's curriculum that ignored not only the special gifts that their children brought to the classroom but also the entire heritage of the African civilization. They thought that the school should hire more African-American teachers so that the staff would become more sensitive and aware of Black children's special talents. They talked about the rich heritage of the African nations, the many languages and cultures on the continent and the half-truths taught in the name of American civilization. They wanted to know how teachers taught and talked about slavery and what they told the children about the civil rights era. They wanted to know how the teachers corrected students' use of language in class and on written work. They argued that if their children's special talents and heritage were recognized, they would perform better in school. At times they seemed angry but not so angry that they were mad and mean. They talked in reasonable tones and with a sense of passion and urgency about their children's education.

The other group seemed to represent the majority of parents. It included both Black and White parents and it outnumbered the other group. Many of these parents said that they too agreed that the curriculum could be more representative of the variety of cultural heritages represented in the school. But they added that there was a real world out there and that this school should help their kids get ready for that real world. They said that learning was hard work. The teachers ought to be challenging students and one way to do this was to give their kids homework every night. But rather than hard work and challenging material, what they saw at the school were low expectations for Black and White kids alike. They appeared to agree with the other parents that the schools' current approach seemed geared for "poor" kids and they wanted to know why the staff wasn't using materials that challenged their children and covered the same material that was covered in the suburbs. The people out in the suburbs knew that stuff and their kids learned it. Why wasn't the staff at Rosa Parks teaching their children this material? They wanted the schools to teach their children what they needed to know so that they could get a job or go to college. What kind of skills were they learning that would help prepare them for a job or college? The published scores clearly indicated that students at Rosa Parks were not doing well. Right now their kids didn't like school and they seemed to be learning very little. These parents didn't want the staff to sugar coat the learning. They expected the teachers to push their children to learn the same material and the same skills that were being taught in the suburbs.

Sally was interested to see the staff's reaction to the parents' concerns. Given the talk she had heard in the teachers' lounge Sally thought she would see staff members squirm and wiggle in their seats. Frequently, she had heard teachers say that these kids don't want to learn. The teachers also seemed to believe that as long as the parents didn't hear about any behavior problems they didn't really care about what went on in school. When they did hear about problems the teachers thought that the parents just threatened the kids with the back of their hand or worse. In class, the teachers seemed to feel that they were successful if the children sat in their desks quietly, didn't make any undue noise and performed the tasks for that day. It wasn't that the teachers didn't care, it just seemed that they focused their efforts on maintaining order in the classroom so that the day went by smoothly.

But what frustrated Sally was that many of the other teachers just didn't react to the parents' concerns. They sat and listened. They nodded politely. And they said that they would try to make some changes in the classroom. Joe Riley seemed eager to move the meeting along as quickly as possible. He hadn't called the meeting, the parents had. He seemed to be on the edge of his seat the entire evening. Finally, Sally spoke up, a bit tentative and nervous and not quite sure what she would say. "I hear what you all are saying, and it seems to me that everyone is unhappy with the school's curriculum. But if you go down to the textbook storeroom you'll see that we don't have much to work with. The books are all old and outdated and they're in pretty poor shape. The kids think the stuff is all pretty boring and I don't really like what I have to use. It seems that the storeroom is our basic problem." At this point she looked around at the other teachers and saw them nodding, agreeing vigorously. Joe Riley seemed pleased with what she had to say and added: "Yeah, it's a pretty sore sight." Alfred Jones, one of the parents, then spoke: "Well, who's responsible for keeping the materials up to date?" Riley said that was the job of central administration. There was some rumbling among the parents and then Jones said: "Well, that's got to change."

As the evening began to wear on (and wear thin on some teachers and parents), Riley suggested creating a curriculum task force for the school. He wanted to be fair so he said he would ask for volunteers from both groups of parents at the meeting, teachers, and the parents who were unable to attend the meeting. He said that he was sure that Sally would join the group and that he would ask for other teachers' involvement. Before the meeting broke up, Felicia Bannecker, one of the parents, gave the final message of the evening. She said that she didn't think the textbook storeroom was the only source of the school's problems. She said the staff needed to look at not only what they taught but how they taught. And she added that if these problems weren't addressed then she felt that parents should contact the school board and the local paper. If it came to that, the school would have to change whether the staff liked it or not.

When Sally woke up the next morning she wondered what role she would play in this new task force and what it would do to her already very busy days. She was new and she didn't have many close friends among the staff. Given the different messages she had heard the night before she knew that there wasn't going to be any easy resolution to the problems that they faced. But despite this feeling of uneasiness she was excited that something new and different might come about. Maybe they could sell all of the old books off and begin anew. Maybe they could go and visit some of the other high schools she had heard were doing some innovative things with both curriculum and instruction. Sally knew she tended to be an optimist and that the world around her rarely followed the paths of her dreams. But she thought she would pursue them anyway.

READER REACTIONS TO SALLY'S SITUATION
AND THE ISSUES AT RPHS

REACTIONS TO "CURRICULUM AND CULTURE"

In recent years, much has been made of the need for, or the existence of a "multicultural" curriculum. For many, the knowledge that is taught in schools is not neutral or value free but rather contains and expresses particular values. Some individuals argue for a curriculum that centers on the achievements of particular cultural groups (e.g., Asante, 1991/1992), others maintain that our schools and their curricula are already multicultural and need go no further (e.g., Ravitch, 1991), and still others maintain that we need to recognize both the divisions and the similarities that exist in our multiethnic society (e.g., Banks, 1991/1992). In this case study, parents are questioning what knowledge, what curriculum, is appropriate for their children. We also hear about teachers who have settled for quiet classrooms, for whom the curriculum needs to be a quiet one. In this realm questions about culture, content, and instruction abound.

Content, Culture, and Instruction

In a democratic society, the content and instruction of public schools should enrich rather than divide distinct cultural groups. Unfortunately, many individuals do not perceive that schools actually perform that democratic function. In fact, many believe that both content and instruction serve to distance rather than engage many students, especially those of color. For many people, focusing on the curriculum without considering instruction, or highlighting instruction without examining the curriculum, leaves a gap that has to be reconsidered. To these individuals, both instruction and curriculum are important. And for others, a consideration of culture, content, and instruction requires that we rethink our conceptions of education and schooling and attend to student learning in a much more vital and engaging fashion.

> Sally's situation is one that is unfortunately very common. There are two problems that I see as in need of immediate reconciliation at Rosa Parks High School. The books/supplies issue is an obvious money problem. There is often little to be done in this area. Sometimes the enormous costs will hinder learning, however the other problem—that of delivery or style of teaching can be remedied.
> The school—having a mixture of both Black and White students—has a need to provide curriculum that caters to all. The delivery of teaching in this school should be sensitive to the fact that there is a diverse group of students, being sure not to favor or discriminate.

Sally has an opportunity to change things and make education in her school, what it should be. I too would be excited.

—Prospective Teacher

The materials that the teachers have to use are important, but they're not the only problem. The main problem is that the teachers have low expectations of the students based on their social class. Keeping order should not be a sign of accomplishment in teaching. I agree with the African-American parents who want their children's special talents and history acknowledged. But this should apply to *all* the students. All the students should be appreciated in terms of the talents they possess. Those who are gifted in art or music or shop should be encouraged to develop those talents into skills that can be used in the "real world." Students who want to go to college should be adequately prepared. A multicultural approach to literature and social studies should be implemented—especially African culture since it is one of the "dominant" cultures in the school and because the school is named after Rosa Parks. But multiculturalism should include other cultures, too.

—Prospective Teacher

This strikes me as addressing a lot of problems that worry me about teaching, especially regarding what perspective(s) the curriculum should present so as not to favor or exclude anyone racially, culturally, or by gender. I still don't know if an all-encompassing curriculum is a feasible goal, given time restraints daily and per semester. This situation has so many aspects to it, I think to deal effectively with it, one would have to break it down into separate issues. For instance, a task force to deal with the outdated textbooks is one good place to start, but I imagine that textbooks are outdated because money to stay up to date on books is minimal. Teaching styles should be addressed: What could be done to allow various races and cultures to utilize their talents most effectively? Curriculum could be addressed, too. Maybe the homework issue could be tackled by assigning work in which a student deals with a classroom topic from a different gender of race or culture's point of view.
What about the students? They should have been represented as well at this meeting. What do they want, not want, like, dislike?
This meeting would have made me nervous, too! But there are too many inputs at play in this situation to call for a catch-all answer—I think!

—Prospective Teacher

It is difficult to tell where the real problem at Rosa Parks High School lies. SAT scores are not always a good example of how much children are learning. However, since it is our nationwide measurement it would prove that there is a problem in the [school].

The concern of the parents seems to target in on the problem much better than the teachers' concern [with] mainly materials. I think the most important aspect of learning is being able to relate it to yourself. If the classroom is not considering the types of students and their interests, then the class is unable to learn. It is important to discover childrens' likes to help get them excited about learning and their broader knowledge by relating new things to them. The comment on learning about their own cultural heritage really hits home. Children need to learn about their own culture as well as the "traditional American culture." This way they can compete in the American rat race! Perhaps even a class in how to take tests like the SAT [would be good].

I also feel that it is important to review schools' materials more often than every 15 to 20 years. The more outdated the material is the harder it is to relate it to the students. There is also the need for more parent–teacher involvement. Without these conferences how can the teacher really know how this hits home with the students.

This is not a small instance—it seems to happen everywhere. Perhaps there is more of a need for teachers to review and revise their curriculum every year.

—Prospective Teacher

There are, of course, many cultural arguments embedded within Sally's story. Most of these arguments center around the curriculum. But I want to go beyond this and focus on human learning. I do not think battles of curriculum are a waste of time. Just the opposite. They are battles worth fighting. I *do* believe a diverse cultural point of view needs to be presented in school curricula. I *do* believe that more teachers of color will help serve as role models to an increasingly non-White school population. As much as I believe all of this and as much as I am willing to work (fight) for change, the battles over curriculum and personnel miss the mark.

Schooling is textbook, curricula, and standardized testing. Learning is about being human. All humans learn. Not all humans do well in school. The curriculum is like a gear in a big institutional machine. If the machine doesn't work, we want to replace the gear. But maybe it isn't the gear. Maybe it's the entire machine. It isn't the curriculum that fails Sally's school, it is outmoded metaphors of learning. Students sit passively in their desks. Order, above all else, must be maintained. These teachers could have the best multicultural text available and if students sit passively, if order and quiet are still paramount virtues, then the texts will fail, maybe not today, but in a week, 2 months—whenever the newness wears off, the books will fail.

Curriculum cannot keep pace with the constant change of culture. This is proven today by map makers and geography textbooks as they try to keep pace with the changes [around the world]. But human learning—learning based on hands-on, *real* experience—is constant. The core of Sally's problem lies with her definition of learning.

Sally is interesting as well in this story. As a new teacher, she feels something is wrong, but literally can't speak out. Institutional pressures will not allow her. To speak out at the meeting was an important step for Sally. She began to assert her individuality. But, alas, it is a false individuality for she is challenging something that is designed to be challenged: curriculum textbooks. The veteran teachers have seen many textbooks committees come and go. But had Sally challenged the "how" of learning, rather than the "what," she would have met with serious problems. Challenging the metaphors of learning is challenging the total systems of education, from desk arrangements to assessment, from an emphasis on order to a reliance on grades.

The metaphors of human learning are so entrenched within our society that they cut across all economic groups. That is why some parents wanted to cover the materials used in the suburbs. As long as we are engaged in definitions of "proper" curriculum, real change will not occur. Until we focus our discussions on student-centered approaches to schooling, students of all cultures will lose.

—Administrator

Difficult Students and Parents

For others, the problem lies not so much with antiquated views of learning or an inadequate attention to curriculum and instruction, but rather with the parents and the children who attend the schools. According to this view, poverty breeds contempt and poor behavior. In these situations the teacher needs to put forth a valiant effort—at least more than is required in settings where parents and students are perceived as being more supportive.

Sally was correct in observing that no one was happy with the school's curriculum—especially the students. I think, however, that the other teachers were right—many of the parents probably could care less. However, when working with poor materials—both the books and students who come from families where education isn't stressed—an extra effort has to be made to achieve what is effortlessly achieved in a suburban high school. It seems to me that it would be more difficult to teach to students whose parents didn't know or hadn't even been exposed to the stuff being taught in the school. The student sees that his or her parent(s) survived without all this garbage, and why should they bother to learn it. Parents also have difficulty helping children at home, and question the validity if they themselves didn't learn it.

—Prospective Teacher

I think that schools need to have parents participate in all facets of education. A curriculum task force is a good idea. I think this issue connects with the public school voucher [proposals]. Parents should be able to choose where they send their kids to school and how their tax dollars are spent. Right now public education is monolithic. If a parent dislikes her child's school—but can't afford a private school—the child is out of luck. Opponents of the voucher system claim that it will increase economic, racial, and social stratification but an overwhelming majority of minority group members support it.

—Prospective Teacher

School Staff, the Community, and Student Achievement

Others react in a manner that lays much less blame on the parents and the students. For these individuals the problem lies not so much with the parents and students but rather in the complex situation in which teachers, parents, and students find themselves. Schooling is a community endeavor and one for which the community should take responsibility. Parents, teachers, and students need to accept this shared responsibility and act in educational ways that will be challenging and rewarding.

It definitely sounds like this school needs some stirring up. It seems as if all the parties are unhappy: teachers, students, and parents. I think that the two groups of parents described have valid complaints. Both the curriculum and instruction at the school need to be changed. However, it's easy to point fingers and blame teachers for education's problems. If the community has the right to complain about the educational system, they too have the responsibility to make constructive changes with it. Already overburdened teachers need support, time, and knowledge for changing curriculum. Much of this support needs to come from the community.
I have observed teachers who appear apathetic with their teaching. I don't think that this apathy comes from a disregard for the students' education but rather reflects an individual who does not have the time or energy to make necessary changes. Therefore, all suffer.

—Student Teacher

I think Sally was brave to take a chance at criticizing the school's storeroom! But taking that risk worked out for her and helped the meeting move in a positive direction. I hope she can maintain her idealism as she helps with the curriculum task force. It's a great opportunity for her since the need is so great and now there is support from the principal and other teachers. The school will benefit from her attitudes and initiative.

Considering the problems at Rosa Parks High School, the parents are most likely correct about the students not being challenged and given the same opportunities as the suburban schools. Hiring an African-American teacher would definitely help. However, the current teachers should not assume that parents do not care or that students do not care about their futures. If students are performing poorly in school, teachers need to reflect on *themselves*, not blame the poor performance on the students. This reflection needs to include *how* they're teaching and *what* they're teaching. But the teachers need support as well especially from the district with new ideas, materials, classes, staff development and activities (especially multicultural). Once this happens, attitudes should improve which hopefully would carry over to students and parents.

—Student Teacher

Money talks, and parents with money talk a lot, as I have found in the upper middle-/middle-class school that I'm in. There's a big difference among this school and the other lower class schools I've been in, in terms of attitudes of teachers, accountability for teachers and students, expectations and materials. Our professional library is current and well-stocked. We have the materials we need to work with students and our staff is constantly seeking professional development opportunities. Sally was right in speaking up about the school's storeroom, but frankly I'm surprised she didn't get shot down by the administration. But now she's taken on a task that is a full-time job in itself and she will be run into the ground with that plus her regular teaching load. There's a high price to pay for being a maverick and the question often is: "But is it worth it? And for how long?" Good luck, Sally!

—Teacher

General Reactions to Sally's Situation

According to other readers, Sally needs to continue her efforts and she needs to ensure that her work is informed by a sense of realism and idealism. She must try to understand her school within the context of both the city and the suburbs and she must not stop trying to improve the materials and instruction. Seeing her school within this larger context should help her understand some of the obstacles that she will encounter. And enhancing the educational setting will mean focusing on her students, connecting—through instruction—her students with meaningful curriculum.

Concern with test scores is the wrong concern. Those test scores do not capture the richness of what might be (but probably isn't) going on in the classroom. However, other issues need to be addressed: the outdated, second-rate materials and the low expectations of the teachers. These issues suggest the failures of the district, pointing to institutional constraints, and also to the teachers who probably represent the privileged in society, the educated, the middle-class. It sounds like this is another clash between the privileged and the not privileged.

Another point both groups missed reared up when the parents demanded that Rosa Parks High School offer the same material the suburbs use. First there is a myth at play here. The material in the suburbs is not standard or consistent. Taking a look at the literature taught in various secondary classrooms illustrates this. Even though there are pieces of literature that *tend* to be taught more often, the literature "canon" of the high school varies greatly and is a hotly debated issue. True, the material of the suburbs might be in better shape and more up to date, but the ideal of meeting the standard is a wrong one. If one goal of good teaching is to bring the curriculum and the student together, then the materials need to represent, reflect, and address the students in different settings.

Laying the blame solely on the feet of the central administration is next to scapegoating. A creative teacher with access to either a copier or a transparency maker can work around this problem.

Three cheers for Felicia Bannecker who confronted the real issues: the need for everyone to take responsibility for the current situation. As a parent, she is taking responsibility for showing up at the meeting and voicing her opinion. Also, three cheers for Sally and her optimistic perspective. The nature of education must be one of idealism and optimism. After all, we are looking at the future and if we do so with the limits of negativity, we need to step aside and let others move into the profession. I do suspect, however, that Sally's vision of the problem might be limited—that she needs to be aware of the power of the privileged as it restricts the less privileged.

—High School Teacher

The parent who "closed" the meeting was absolutely right—it's not the materials and the content alone—the process of teaching (and the embedded messages) is what really counts. The school could replace its outdated texts, and still not improve its teaching.

Sally, as a member of the task force, would do well to observe and address the objectives of the staff. If the main objective is to have a smooth, orderly day, then here is the root of the problem. As a newer teacher, she could be a fresh breeze for some who are set in their ways. Many agreed the books were useless, but none had taken any initiative.

The African-American parents made a good argument for representation. However, the school should be wary of overrepresenting them in an effort to "make up for lost time." It would be ideal to add in the interests of the African American's and every other "minority" group as well, and the balance should be equal. To give one group overrepresentation is just the same (although in the reverse) as keeping Whites in possession of the majority of representation.

—Student Teacher

Sally has reason to feel optimistic. Her own concerns are going to be acted on, hopefully. That is, the storeroom materials are going to be evaluated and she may have something to say about changing them. She should pay attention to what's going on with the other teachers, though. The fact that they have reduced their classrooms to babysitting sessions and aren't motivated to improve them seems to be a common occurrence in American schools. Maybe it's easier to write off your students as unwilling to lean, and parents as disinterested, than it is to change yourself as a teacher. Sally should be careful not to let herself slide into their patterns and become an obstacle rather an aid to her students' learning.
I'm not sure how much of what's happening is due to the fact that Rosa Parks High School is culturally mixed. But it's probably got a lot to do with money. And maybe even more to do with lack of leadership. Curriculum problems can be solved to some extent if there's money to replace outdated materials. Poor teaching can be resolved if teachers are motivated, like Sally, by either better pay or personal performance standards. Sally should probably try to get the school to address the other teachers' attitudes if she really wants to see some change in the quality of education at Rosa Parks.

—ESL Teacher

The public meeting which was featured in this case study served well to open lines of communication and to break initial stereotypes. Sally played a key role by acknowledging parental concerns as justified, and expressing her own concerns. While limited curriculum resources may be one problem, the issues these people face go far beyond simple curriculum resources. The question must be asked: Why are the books so outdated? Some likely explanations are money problems, lack of awareness that there is a problem, or lack of motivation for change. People's preconceived ideas about others are deeply ingrained and guide one's perceptions of the world without conscious awareness. Teacher expectations of students greatly effect their performances and the language we use delivers subtle messages to others about our expectations and attitudes. This meeting highlighted that neither teachers nor parents matched the stereotypes. Hopefully by setting up a committee to start talking about the issues, lines of communication and understanding will be developed.

— Teacher

READER REACTIONS TO "CURRICULUM AND CULTURE"

SUMMARY AND ADDITIONAL QUESTIONS

As a society we have become more aware of the function, the role, and the importance of knowledge. Some have argued (see, e.g., Apple, 1993; Bourdieu & Passeron, 1977) that certain knowledge represents the "cultural capital" that students use to make good investments later in their educational career and postschool lives. These individuals maintain that in our society some are granted access to that cultural capital while others are denied. Other commentators maintain that we are a society that is "culturally illiterate" (see, e.g., Finn, 1991; Hirsch, 1988). According to these individuals, all the talk about multicultural curricula only serves to dilute the binding function of knowledge in our society. We need traditional knowledge taught to all and it must be taught well. Still others base their claims about what we should do based on the perceived "needs" of the student. If our schools aren't working then we should change them. If students need a curriculum that is more related to the world around them—then we need to give it to them. These represent varying perspectives on the issues raised by the "Curriculum and Culture" case study. Here, we identify a few questions that develop and pursue reactions identified thus far.

1. Is there any body of knowledge or set of experiences to which all students should be exposed? In a democratic society should we expect that students leave school with any shared understandings? How would you describe those shared understandings, that body of knowledge, or set of experiences?
2. John Goodlad (1984), Jean Anyon (1980), and Jonathan Kozol (1991) present persuasive evidence that our public schools offer distinct types of knowledge and experiences to different groups of students—based primarily on student's class, race, and culture. What do you make of this type of curriculum differentiation?
3. Linda McNeil (1986) noted the manner in which students and teachers bargain for a controlled and manageable class. What is the effect on the curriculum and on a student's education when classroom control, in the form of quiet classrooms, becomes the overriding goal?
4. As a teacher you walk into a school district that has elaborated a set of curricular goals. Is it the teacher's job to incorporate curricular elements that are not identified in the district's goals?

INTRODUCTION TO CASE 3

In Case 3, we explore further the notion of a cultural identity through examining the ways in which a teacher's cultural identity and his or her professional identity mesh and conflict. As we underscored in "School and Home," individuals have cultural identities. Teachers, given their professional responsibilities and endeavors, also have professional identities. Teachers' professional identities vary. Some teachers are more discipline-based, whereas others are more child-focused. Some are more concerned with content, whereas others emphasize process. And certainly some attempt to bring the emphases of disciplinary understandings and the focus on students together and to integrate content and process. (For a further elaboration of distinct professional identities see the first volume in this series, *Reflective Teaching: An Introduction,* Zeichner & Liston, 1996.) Beginning teachers are, in many ways, frequently just becoming aware of their own cultural identities and in the process of articulating and formulating their professional identities. Attempting to create an educational and powerful combination of these two identities can be a major endeavor. Another task that confronts some teachers is the idea that in a multicultural world some cultures and some cultural identities are privileged and that the experience of schooling may add to the privilege of some cultures while it detracts from others. In "Teachers and Cultural Identities," we explore these and other issues.

CASE 3: "TEACHERS AND CULTURAL IDENTITIES"

This was going to be Linda's first year of teaching. She had looked for a job in her hometown but couldn't find one. She had searched within a radius of 50 miles and still she didn't have any luck. But the first time that she went past and just a bit west of the Appalachian Mountains she was offered a job during the interview. She was going to teach in a town of about 80,000 people. "Her" school was in one of the poorer sections of town and she would be teaching first grade. Few if any of her students would be White and middle class. Almost all of her students were going to be poor and either Black or Hispanic; a few would be White. It was going to be a very different setting for Linda. She had grown up in a solidly White, middle-class neighborhood. Her mother was and still is an elementary teacher and her father is the manager of a business supply office. She had attended public school, one that was predominantly White and middle class. There were a few Black students in her high school but not many. Some of the Black students were bussed into the school while a few other Black families lived in her neighborhood. But she never really got to know those kids. Although White and Black kids had attended her school they never seemed to mix. Now most of the faces she would see this fall would be Black and brown.

In her teacher education program a few of the professors had made a big thing of multicultural education and cultural differences among teachers and students. In fact one of the professors had her entire class talk about their own "cultural" identity. At first, that seemed odd because there were only two Blacks in the class but as the week proceeded Linda began to think about her own cultural identity. There were two class sessions that left a big impression on her. In one class session, a professor of bilingual education taught the class in Spanish. The first time she went through the material no one understood her. Linda remembered feeling a gamut of emotions. At first she was lost and bewildered. She then began to look to other students for help. After experiencing further frustration, she began to feel angry—angry at the instructor and her own inability with Spanish. The instructor then taught the same lesson a second time, speaking more slowly and deliberately, utilizing pictures and visual aides, and elaborating key ideas. Linda left that class session with a vivid experience of what it might feel like to have a language other than English as her primary tongue.

In another class session, the professor talked at length about the "assumed" and unacknowledged privileges that Whites seem to have in our society. She read from a paper by Peggy McIntosh (1988) about how as a White individual she could pretty much assume that:

> ... I can go shopping alone most of the time, pretty well assured that I will not be followed or harassed.
>
> ... I can turn on the television or open to the front page of the paper and see people of my race widely represented.
>
> ... I can talk with my mouth full and not have people put this down to my color.
>
> ... I can be pretty sure that my children's teachers and employers will tolerate them if they fit school and work place norms; my chief worries about them do not concern others' attitudes toward their race.
>
> ... I am never asked to speak for all people of my racial group.
>
> ... I can be late to a meeting without having the lateness reflect on my race. (pp. 5–9)

The professor argued that Black or Hispanic individuals usually could not make these assumptions. Although this made sense, it seemed that most of her professors were too liberal. They tended to blame society (whatever that was) for all of the public schools' problems. They didn't seem to talk about or at least give the same emphasis to the fact that people, regardless of race or ethnic background, need to work hard in order to make good in today's world. Sometimes Linda thought that the university people forgot about this need for hard work. And they certainly seemed to forget that some schools had lots of White, middle-class children attending also.

But she wasn't going to be teaching White, middle-class students and so her thoughts turned to her recent field experiences and her student teaching, settings that had included minority children. She remembered her difficulty talking about the minority students in those classrooms. It always seemed to be a touchy topic. When teachers did broach the topic, it seemed that she heard lots of stories about how "those kids'" homes and backgrounds just don't support school. Linda heard stories of single mothers with children who had several different fathers. She heard talk about "crack" babies. It seemed that when problems arose the staff wondered if the child was a crack or drug baby. When the same types of problems arose with some of the White students it was rare to hear any one mention drugs as a possible problem. Many of the minority kids seemed so far behind most of the White students.

As a student teacher, Linda tried to get to know all of her students. It seemed that her conversations with many of her White children went smoothly and she got a lot of information from them. But with all too many of her Black and Hispanic children, especially the boys, she wasn't able to learn much about them. When she would ask questions about their family or neighborhood she frequently got blank stares or quizzical looks as a response. That happened when she was teaching, too. Sometimes in the middle of the lesson she would stop and ask students a question to check for understanding or to ask them to repeat what she had just said. Many times she got no response from her Hispanic or Black children. On the other hand, Linda observed that some of her minority students were definitely talented kids. Outside of the classroom many of her minority students interacted with each other and adults in lively, challenging, and intellectually demanding ways. This contrasted sharply with their behavior during lessons. It seemed to Linda that something or someone was to blame for the poor achievement of her minority kids. Her university instructors always talked about "society," whereas her parents had talked about the importance of the family and family values. Linda didn't feel like she could blame her students—they were too young. And she didn't accept other teachers' views that these students were basically dull or unmotivated. Something was wrong somewhere and she didn't know what to do about it.

One thing Linda did know was that there were probably very few simple answers or resolutions to these issues. She wanted to make her new classroom a friendly, warm, challenging, and secure place. She felt that she needed to find out more about her students and not be such a strange presence in their lives. She recalled that during her student teaching, her cooperating teacher, Beth, had started to make home visits. Beth had come back from one of her visits intrigued and invigorated. She had visited William's home and for the first time, Beth related, she got a little better sense of what school meant to William and his mother. She had arranged the visit a week ahead of time and William's mother, Louise, had to cancel twice. On the phone, Louise persisted in wanting to know what kind of problems William was causing and why Beth wanted to talk to her in person. When Beth arrived at their house, the first thing Louise asked was, "So what kind of trouble has William been making?" Beth repeated that she just wanted to meet William and his family at a place other than school and hoped that with this first meeting they would then be able to talk more easily about William's progress and his problems. Louise responded: "Well, this is the first time I've heard about teachers coming into your house without there being a problem." She then apologized for canceling the two earlier meetings. It seemed that William's little sister had been sick and the health clinic was only open after school hours.

William showed Beth the room he shared with his older brother and Beth talked with Louise about the schoolwork that she would be giving William. Louise remarked once more that it seemed strange for someone to come knocking on her door before a problem occurred. She also told Beth that school had not been her most enjoyable experience. Although she had enjoyed elementary school, by the time she got to high school it seemed her teachers were just babysitting and telling her what she couldn't do. After awhile she started to act up and after that she just wanted to get out. Louise talked about the books and math problems that she gave William and how they enjoyed making up stories together. Her message to William was that he had better do good in school because that was how he was going to make good in the world.

Beth wasn't quite sure what she had expected from this meeting. But she now saw William and his family in less distant, more familiar terms. Linda remarked that Louise's views of schools and institutions seemed like places that bothered you rather than helped you. In contrast, Linda's parents had always seen schools as places that were there to serve their children. When a problem or obstacle occurred they walked up to the school to talk about it. Louise didn't seem to have that experience. And so Linda started thinking that she would try and tackle home visits her first year.

Linda also wondered whether she might be taking on too much. She worried that she needed to figure out what to do in the classroom before she figured out what to do outside of the classroom. She worried that she just didn't have much experience with the students who would fill her classroom this fall. Her parents had raised her to be fair and not prejudiced. But Linda knew that when she drove from her predominantly White, middle-class neighborhood to her school where she was one of the few White faces in the street, she felt nervous. Although a part of her wanted to ignore the fact that all of her students' lives and experiences were different from hers, she still wanted to find out all about those differences because she felt that in many ways many similarities also existed. She believed that by knowing about these similarities and differences she would be better able to meet the varied needs of her students and to make the kind of instructional connections that would help them. She was certain that it would make her a better teacher. She was anxious and excited. That, she thought, seemed to be her basic and never changing reaction to teaching.

READER REACTIONS TO LINDA'S ISSUES

REACTIONS TO "TEACHERS AND CULTURAL IDENTITIES"

Talk about culture and teaching can be kept at a distance. This case study seems to reduce that distance. It may seem odd for many White, middle-class individuals to think of themselves as having a cultural identity. But a certain degree of shared norms, practices, and beliefs are held by Whites as well as people of color. The assumptions that we carry around with us, those created by our advantages and our past injuries, affect how we see students in our classrooms and schools. If we are White and have had little interaction with students of color we will be guided by assumptions and beliefs that have little basis in actual personal practice. Our professional and cultural identities are formed before and while we are in the classroom. They affect how we teach and who we teach. Unfortunately, we live in a society that has not taught its members how to talk productively about differences or how to help children deal with those differences and to see the similarities. For teachers, this is a task of a rather large order; one that seems fraught with uncertainty and, at times, rewarded with a sense of fulfillment. It can be an anxious and uncomfortable time.

Reflections on the Personal Side

Most of us, if we are honest, will admit that dealing with the ethnic and cultural issues that face teachers today is a very large challenge. Whether one ends up teaching in a homogeneous or heterogeneous setting, issues of culture and race will be present. Anxiety and discomfort seem to be the prevailing personal reactions, along with a sense of personal integrity and vision.

> *I* am anxious and excited. There are times when I get quite excited by the idea of teaching because I do believe that teachers can make an impact for the good in each student's life. Here though, lies the anxiety. How can I make this important contribution? How am I going to get through to each of my students? Am I going to forget to look at situations from both sides? There seems to be a great deal of important factors to consider, and I fear that I will overlook some important aspect of the situation and do worse than just not help my student—I fear putting them in a hole.
>
> I know that these are not new fears and that I'm certainly not the first or only person to feel this way. I also know that all that I can do is my best and that there will be times when this won't be enough. But I know that I can try to

fix the things I break, or bend, and through a concern for appreciation of other people's worlds, I can be a better teacher.

—Prospective Teacher

This story backs my conviction that I must leave [this university town] immediately. Here I don't come into contact with the variety of cultures and races that I think is important for me [so that I can learn] to be completely comfortable with people who are in many, many ways different from most [of the people in this town].

Even though Linda has terrific intentions, I think her students will probably suffer because of her lack of contact with different cultures and races. In my opinion, no schooling can compensate for actual contact (immediate, continuous contact).

… I have noticed that I am now often uncomfortable around people of a different race than me, although I have had friends who were of different races when I lived in other cities. … I *really hate* this about myself and am convinced that I must somehow rebuild my social contact with other cultures and races either by moving to, or working in, or attending school in a much more "mixed" community.

Being comfortable with all sorts of kids is a prerequisite to being the sort of teacher I want to be. As well as working hard in my academic classes, I need to work equally hard on my person.

—Prospective Teacher

Searching for Commonalities

Some individuals read Linda's case study and underscored the need to search for the commonalities, the threads, that tie us together. In an era in which differences are both celebrated and feared, looking for the ties that bind us together as humans or as democratic citizens can be a way to emphasize our collective orientations. When we look at others we frequently see "others"— not people who share essential and integral human experiences. Teaching seems to require that we see situations from a student's perspective. If we don't recognize what we share with our students it will be difficult to teach well. The following reactions highlight the commonalities that exist among us.

Linda's experiences seem to be shaking the foundation of her beliefs, values, and overall outlook on life, which I feel is good. I wish more people in the majority culture could experience what it feels like to be a "minority." She's finding out that she feels there are universals which connect us all as human beings, and I think that her new found empathy will make her a much better teacher. People can read multicultural literature until hell freezes over, but if they never interact with people from different cultures, they'll never truly "get it."

—First-Year Teacher

I feel frustrated that treating people differently because of their race is still even an issue in our society. Regardless of differences in race, sex, and culture, human beings share many of the same basic needs. Our culture is very much part of who we are but not our essence. Unfortunately, these characteristics often define how society treats and labels us.

I think that Linda's attitude is great. I imagine that home visits can be very intimidating. However, they are important in making connections between the home and school. What a positive way to begin the school year, meeting families with the goal of making connections versus only talking with the family when there are problems. Home visits are also an effective way of reducing feelings of alienation with all three parties: student, home, and teacher.

—Student Teacher

The Need to Talk About Differences

But it seems that in order to note the commonalities and make the connections we also need to recognize and talk about the differences that exist between us. Ignoring differences does not do justice to who we are. Talking about those differences, when differences can divide and antagonize, is not a simple or uncomplicated affair. These next reactions highlight the need to approach and talk about differences.

I can relate to Linda's concerns. I, too, grew up in middle-class suburbia outside Detroit, MI. There is a large Black minority, a large Arabic minority, but not so many Hispanics. My middle and high school experience was one big homogeneous group. I don't consider myself prejudiced and feel I am accepting of people for their character, not their sexual orientation, religious background, or race. However, as glorified a picture as I may paint of myself, I realize that I may not be able to relate to the kids in the manner that a teacher of that minority status might. How is this solved? I don't know.

Concerning Linda's worries about home visits, especially when she worried "that she just didn't have much experience with the students who would fill her classroom," she is headed in the right direction. If she is a fair person, she can learn from the students and parents, even if she stumbles a bit. I believe that differences are important. To say that we are all human underneath our skin color/religious preference/some other minority status simplifies it just too much. The differences that are present define us, make up our history, and structure our lifestyles. When these differences become disruptful or destructive it is time for intervention and to look to ways we are similar. Diversity can also be a wonderful teaching tool.

—Teacher

Many of these issues I relate to because her background is similar [to mine]. … It is important to see the positive outlook that she shows at the end of this case study. To be able to approach her classroom knowing that differences lie ahead is important, but even more important is her approach to find out what things she has in common with the children. I think this is a great approach since she will be addressing the ethnic issue openly and not holding her feelings in, and being "ashamed" of them.

—Prospective Teacher

It's obvious that there is *much* anxiety over cultural, racial, and ethnic differences for the student and the teacher. There really is no "answer" or solution to these types of problems. Maybe addressing her anxiety and the anxiety of her students right off the bat would help. These types of problems are quite valid. I think any "soon to be teacher"—Black or White—will experience these feelings. … It is very important for the teacher to know or get in touch with the feelings of [all] students.

—Prospective Teacher

I can identify with Linda. What makes me upset is that no one can ever talk about the instructor's problems when [he or she] is dealing with [difficulties concerning] racial and ethnic diversity. Everything is always internalized. What is also frustrating is that even though a teacher, like Linda, may have the best intentions to discover the similarities between the differences, you know she will have problems because she hasn't first dealt with the differences openly. It also bothers me that she is still commuting from her White middle class neighborhood to the poorer area of the city that her students live in. She always will have the solace of her home after school.

—Prospective Teacher

Linda seems to have a very healthy attitude to begin exploring cultural differences. She had been exposed to issues of cultural identity in her university classes, yet they did not seem to take on meaning for her until she was faced with real students who were different. To me, this emphasizes the need for an experiential context to lessons. Once students are presented with both knowledge and experience, they still need support to start making bridges to apply this learning. This need for assistance may be especially true in issues of culture where the differences are so grounded in differing world views and experiences. Also, cultural differences as they play out in our society are so complex, they cannot be simply addressed in class. Linda recalls useful university lessons as she recognizes the application to help understand cultural similarities and differences. She will pursue these lessons because she is invested in finding ways to better reach her students' needs. This curiosity, respect, and sincere interest will serve her well in working with people who are different.

—Experiential Educator

Instructional and Cultural Issues

We can talk about and recognize both the differences and the commonalities that exist within our schools but unless we find ways to make the instructional connections with those differences and commonalities we will not be teaching well. This next set of reactions talks to the need to recognize the instructional part of all of this.

I think Linda is on the right track about familiarizing herself with the different cultures in her classroom in order to reach her kids more effectively. The home visits worked for her cooperating teacher to understand parents' views of education as well as learning about the students' cultures. Hopefully, it will be the same for Linda so she can figure out why she gets blank stares sometimes in the classroom. Is there a difference in dialect? Are the children not understanding her jargon? Are they raised to be submissive and nonverbal to a teacher or authority figure?

It sounds like Linda has a positive attitude towards her future class. She seems open-minded and well prepared for a challenge. These are great assets! Hopeful she won't slip into the stereotype that minority students tend to fail due to their race. It doesn't sound like she will.

—Student Teacher

Linda is on the right track. She has a moment of potential loss of momentum when she thinks she's taking on too much—that she has to decide on the classroom issues before she moves outside. In a situation so new to her, and therefore so fraught with learning opportunities, it will be crucial for her to work from the outside in. So often, when the reverse tactic is employed, it seems the right, safe thing to do. But really it sets up a precedent of imposition. When the "authority" figure implements a plan to meet a populations' needs, without knowledge of what those needs are, they deservedly are viewed as inattentive to those needs—as lacking compassion, as self-interested. This is especially the case when the "authority" figure does not represent, and has no experience with, the culture being served. In fact, her efforts to "take on too much" now ought to doubly repay her later, when her newfound knowledge will allow her to facilitate concrete success for her students.

—Student Teacher

Linda's Teacher Education

Some people's reactions highlight the role that Linda's education played in her approach to these issues. They note the need to use at a later date what may initially seem inappropriate or unnecessary material.

Well, I think Linda has an open mind about what her responsibilities should be. Although it is difficult to be put in a different situation (moving from a White suburb to the Appalachian Mountains), Linda seems somewhat prepared to deal with these cultural differences. Linda's critique of some of her "liberal" professors seems to be common among many students. However, after she is put into an actual teaching situation, the rich/critical information that she received in college helped her make some important decisions. Her *observation* of other teachers' actions, I think, is a good sign of Linda trying to make the best of a different atmosphere and will help her teaching experience for her students and herself.

—Prospective Teacher

Linda's issues don't seem to require any real action on anyone's part other than for Linda to recognize that she is experiencing what a lot of new teachers experience and that her worries actually indicate how dedicated a teacher she will probably be. Hopefully, she will find some other teachers to advise and commiserate with her at her new job. I have a lot of hope for Linda. She has had or learned from several experiences which could be called consciousness-raising: her college classes, student teaching, her cooperating teacher's home visits and reflections about her own upbringing and how it differs from that of other students from other backgrounds. I admire her resolve to come to terms with her students' experiences. If she continues to push herself to address her students' issues and to try new ways of meeting their needs, such as home visits, she'll probably be a very successful teacher.

—ESL Teacher

General Reactions to Linda's Situation

Despite these generally positive reactions to Linda's efforts, a number of individuals feared that Linda would probably not last in her current situation. She seems, many feared, to lack a certain critical awareness. They seem to be saying that although she was "taught" a certain critical awareness, she may not be educated or motivated enough to make significant contributions.

Linda's challenge is probably a common one, although her outlook of sensitivity is probably less typical. My "gut reaction" is to think that Linda will not be teaching in this school long, especially if she can gain a few years of experience, then move elsewhere. Linda's issues as presented here are great and many, but to the extent that Linda is aware of [the] many hurdles she will find ways to be successful in her classroom. It seems to me that her bigger struggle will be finding ways to be successful in her school.

Let's recap the issues as I understand them. Linda is an open-minded rookie beginning her career in an environment racially unlike her and what she's used to. She hopes to treat her students fairly and realizes that both similarities and differences between her students and her experiences exist. Her goal is to make helpful instructional connections based on her students' varied needs. Sounds good.

Let's give Linda credit because she's well meaning and sincere. But I believe Linda's approach is skewed. Communication with parents is important, but how comfortable and enjoyable would a home visit be? "Checking out" a student's home environment may well provide more information that a child is different and the real issue is "How will this child learn in school, in my classroom?" It's a question of motivation, skills, school climate. Linda's time could probably be better spent on creating a positive environment for learning in the classroom regardless of what goes on outside. Of course, every student (and teacher) comes with baggage. But regardless of what it is, the classroom needs to be a safe [and engaging] place for all students to learn. (Hopefully, something relevant [is taught] which, given the Eurocentric nature of much school curriculum, could be a challenge.) Linda will likely do more learning that year than many of her pupils.

Other issues Linda might well ponder in advance [include]: Will her colleagues be resources or is there racial tension between faculty at this school? How will she decide what to teach? What philosophy does she want to permeate her classroom? (Is the teacher the "knower" and are the students the learners? Does fair mean equal, high expectations or do they get lowered for some? Will she be candid about her apprehensions or fearful and hide them? Will there be an atmosphere of community/inclusivity or will vast differences separate learners?) What will she do if she needs help? When Linda says she has difficulty talking to non-White students can she figure out why, and what kind of help she needs? How will she integrate herself into the school and not just be isolated in the classroom?

—Middle School Teacher

The culture of the school and the culture of the home are only too often at odds, as is in Linda's situation. Within the school setting, the teacher and the system hold the power. Individuals or groups who did not have good experiences in school or who do not match the system well stand at a disadvantage in the institutional setting. Linda is to be commended for even thinking about issues of power and privilege. Despite her studies at college, she doesn't seem to understand what it means to not be part of the privileged group and instead seems inclined to blame the individual for weaknesses and deficiencies. Living in this setting is the opportunity for her to confront her own prejudices, if she will only allow herself to be reflective and open. Already she shows signs of fear and nervousness about the cultures around her, fears which I suspect will turn into judgments, harsh ones at that.

—High School Teacher

Linda appears to have really conflicted feelings, both in herself and as a result of her student teaching experience. She seemed willing to keep an open mind, and had been touched by the simulations in her education classes. She also seemed to be trying to see that the different response styles in her ethnically diverse students were not their "fault." (She needs to read Shirley Brice Heath's *Ways with Words*.)

I also worry for Linda. She seems overly sensitive to the ethnic and cultural differences in her students. This seems to be in the forefront when she thinks about them, rather than seeing her students as kids first. I'm afraid that somehow this attitude may convey itself to the students, even if she doesn't want to be "prejudiced."

—Teacher

There seems to be basic differences in the way Linda and her students' families define the word *school*. Linda was raised in a professional, White, upper middle-class setting. *School* embraced the norms embedded within that experience. Linda's students, however, operated from a different set of definitions. School was a totally different experience.

But this contradiction in definitions is too classic. It was exactly the issue that was supposed to be "corrected" by Linda's university "experiences." Although the contrived (as in "not real") experiences of the university made an *impression*, they did not alter Linda's basic definitions of *school*. She felt that her professors were too liberal (aren't they always?). But all the talk about school and conflicting definitions of *school* seem to overlook a basic fact. There hadn't been enough emphasis on *how humans learn*.

Linda saw school as a body of knowledge that needed to be covered in a set amount of time, a *consumer metaphor* of learning. When children of color had problems, they "fell behind." On the other hand, outside of school, Linda's students showed "talents." This was because outside of school, no one prescribes the order of knowledge. Knowledge is a tool that arises out of "real" need.

An interesting distinction can be made here between a "realistic" learning experience and a "real" learning experience. While I don't know what sort of activities Linda employed in her classroom, I can assume that they were "schoolish." The only place these activities would take place would be at school. I would also assume, that occasionally, when Linda was feeling creative, she would engage her kids in what she would view as a "realistic" activity, an activity that had no "real" purpose—like doing research on an assigned topic.

Contrast this with "real" activities; creating a story for a parent's birthday, following a basketball team and keeping track of the statistics, etc. Linda's problems were with her definitions of learning—definitions of how all humans learn— not just with her definitions of *school*.

There is also a big problem with Linda's reasons for teaching where she did. Linda did *not* want to break old definitions. She wanted to stay "home," all safe and comfortable, away from those damn liberals at the university. The *market dictated* Linda's placement, *not* Linda's desire to change society! In short Linda's school choice was formed by *cash*, not *conviction*.

—Administrator

READER REACTIONS TO "TEACHERS AND CULTURAL IDENTITIES"

SUMMARY AND ADDITIONAL QUESTIONS

Teachers have cultural identities and these cultural identities inform and shape a teacher's professional identity. The cultural assumptions that we carry around with us affect how we see others and for teachers these assumptions affect how we see our students and their families. Some individuals view poverty as a sign of personal laziness or ill-fortune. To others, a southern or northern accent may have quite different rings and very distinct "meanings." For others, nonstandard English betokens a cognitive deficit. If a teacher walks into the classroom with these or other assumptions, they will interpret students' interactions in particular ways. Students also interpret teachers' actions and behaviors in ways that the teacher may not understand and certainly doesn't control. It seems that the meanings that are created and inhere in the classroom are affected by numerous factors.

The presence and force of our cultural identities was certainly a salient theme in this case study. Other themes were present and here we attempt both to examine the importance of this notion of cultural identity and other themes.

1. What are the connections among the students' and the teacher's cultural identities and the curriculum and student learning? What can be accomplished by highlighting distinct, and culturally informed, understandings of school subject matter?
2. For some, the call for an enhanced focus on cultural identities seems belabored and educationally irrelevant. What is your sense of this view?
3. Once again we see in this case study an attempt to make connections between the home and the school. Sara Lawrence Lightfoot (1978) maintains that the gap between home and school is large and should be reduced. Others feel that we need to separate the tasks and the responsibilities of the home and the school and leave the gap there. What is your sense?

GENERAL REACTIONS
TO THE THREE CASE STUDIES

Stepping back and looking at all three case studies can encourage one to formulate more general reactions. It is neither easy nor simple to try to garner a general sense but some individuals found it to be a helpful approach. The general reactions are diverse. One individual thinks that although we live in a complicated world, the best a teacher can do is to live his or her life with integrity. Another person believes that the crucial issue among all three case studies has to do with the connection between home and school. And a third person finds that all three case studies stressed the need for teachers to become truly bicultural.

> Schooling has a long way to go to connect with society [in ways that help children], but progress is being made in individual areas, piece by piece. I guess all you can do is to try to make your corner of the world a better place for students to live and grow in, and handle yourself in such a manner that you can still look yourself in the mirror and be happy with what you see there.
> —Teacher

The core issues with this set of case studies is how schools and individual teachers decide to involve parents in the education of their children. These case studies represent a range of interaction with parents from home visits to an "us versus them" mentality where teachers want as little interaction with parents as possible. I think that involving parents as much as is possible and beneficial in the education of their children is absolutely critical in the education of all children, regardless of race or color.

In my experience with classroom environments as a teacher and as a student, it seems apparent that a majority of teachers still persist in trying to keep parents out of their classrooms, as demonstrated in the "Curriculum and Culture" case study. This is the general case in the school I am currently student teaching in. Such an environment creates an unnecessary antagonistic relationship between parents and teachers. Parents not only don't feel involved in what their children are learning and doing, but, all too often, they don't understand this process either.

As for teachers, lack of understanding about each child's home life and lack of communication with parents about the home environment can leave a teacher at a loss about how to reach students. While this is the case with all students, it is intensified with children who are not members of the dominant culture who have different background and heritages than the teacher's. This dilemma became very clear in the case of both Anna and Linda, as they found themselves in the very challenging position of educating and interacting with a majority of children from very different backgrounds than their own. Home visits can provide an amazing way to find out more about children and can go a long way toward creating that vital link between family and school.

In both cases [Anna's and Linda's], but especially in Anna's, more direct involvement in the classroom and in helping their own children through the learning process is needed. From my reading of Anna's case it didn't seem as if she had made much of an effort to involve Estella's parents directly with the classroom before she made her home visit. Both elements are necessary in this equation of assuring equal access and opportunity for each child. Also, making home visits before or early in the year are very useful, such as Linda did. Then home visits become part of laying the ground work for the development of an open and successful classroom environment.

What must always be the essential motive and driving force behind any action or question in the educational setting is what is best for the child. When parents and the child's home life are not explored, understood, and incorporated into the creation of the classroom ethos everyone loses out, but ultimately it is the child who loses the most. There is so much at stake in the education of children, that to not be open to and to not consider all of the elements that make up each child can do nothing more than hinder how and what that child learns. Each child is unique and the most essential parts of who they are develop and are influenced at home, so schools and teachers must make whatever efforts they can to get to know and integrate these elements.

—Student Teacher

The three cases studies here highlight what I perceive as a growing problem in education: the growing cultural gulf between those teaching and those being taught. This is especially true in light of the changing demographics. By the year 2000 the majority of public school students will be Black, Asian, or Hispanic. Yet, the majority of teachers will be White females. Among teachers, there is generally a lack of *biculturalism.* Let me explain the term. As an African American in a White society I am aware of the cultural norms, codes of behavior, expectations, idioms, etc., of the larger predominantly White society. This is necessary in order to move smoothly and upwardly through the system. On the other hand, I am as equally skilled in the cultural norms, codes of behavior, expectations and idioms of Black culture in America. Consequently, I am able to move back and forth with ease and am able to not only sympathize with both cultural orientations but empathize as well.

This is not true of most White Americans. And for the most part it is not an issue until you enter classrooms like the ones Anna, Linda, and Sally did. These three teachers lack the understanding of the codes of behavior, idioms, expectations, past experiences, etc. to make their respective dilemmas less problematic. Take for instance Anna. She speaks some Spanish and is considered bilingual; but she believes she knows something about being a minority in society from her father's experience as a Jew in a Gentile world. But it becomes obvious as Anna is confronted with the issue of how to help Estella exercise her talents to their fullest potential that while she is somewhat bilingual, she is not bicultural. She is not sure how to approach Estella's parents because she is unsure of what their cultural values and expectations are for their daughter. She makes assumptions about where Estella's life will end up and says so to her mother. And makes assumptions about why so many Hispanic girls leave school early.

Despite her good intentions, it appears that Anna has not examined her own teaching practices or those of teachers within the school to find out how they might be impacting Hispanic girls negatively. Nor does it seem that she has made any steps toward becoming literate about Hispanic cultural values. Instead of laying the responsibility solely on the parents to enroll Estella in the gifted option at school, why doesn't she create that sort of academically challenging and engaging environment for all her students within her regular classroom? Why doesn't she seek out the expertise and experience of other Hispanic teachers or community of people? Does she try to educate herself about the variety of cultures that come under the label of "Hispanic" so that she has a better grasp of what it is like for the recent immigrants from Mexico as well as what life is like, both positively and negatively for those Hispanic families who have been in the States for generations?

What bothers me about Anna's hesitation is that if she opts to act either way there is the danger that Estella's parents will be seen as unconcerned about their daughter's education (on the one hand she had to prod them, on the other hand they didn't act at all) and this may reinforce some stereotypes about the lack of value placed on education in the Hispanic home.

But it is Linda's case study that disturbed me the most. Linda's lack of biculturalism saws [into] her classroom interaction. The case study said Linda's "conversations with many of her White children went smoothly and she got a lot of information from them. But with all too many of her Black and Hispanic children, especially the boys, she wasn't able to learn much ... she frequently got blank stares or quizzical looks as a response. That happened when she was teaching too." There was an obvious breakdown in communication and a difference in communication styles, but Linda had no idea what was wrong or how to bridge the gap. The end result of these types of exchanges is usually a misinterpretation of behaviors and all too often a misdiagnosis of learning ability on the part of the teacher. We have all seen a disproportionate number of Black boys suspended, placed in special education classes, and labeled reading disabled. She knows something is wrong, but I suspect that she is looking in the wrong place for the answers. She thinks Beth's method of home visits might work for her. But Linda is handicapped in that even if she does go into the home of a Black parent she does not have the cultural understanding to interpret what she is seeing. She is filtering her experiences inside and outside this classroom through a White, middle-class lens.

Most telling is her comment that "her parents raised her to be fair and not prejudiced." It is not a question of being fair to these children or prejudiced against them. It is a lack of empathy with their cultural experiences. Her uneasiness as she drives from her White, middle-class neighborhood to her inner-city school might be the anxiety that comes from having no cultural reference points. Standard behaviors, linguistic definitions, and value systems she is used to and comfortable with are not the standards she is going to use in this school setting. (Most Black people with similar professional training and credentials aren't "nervous" going from an all Black environment to an all White one because they have learned what is culturally appropriate and inappropriate where Whites are the majority.) I would hope Linda's attempt at learning about the experiences of her students would not be a simple academic exercise, reading about famous Black people like Martin Luther King, etc. She is going to have to go beyond that and immerse herself in the affective part of the Black and Hispanic experience in some meaningful way if she is ever to truly understand her students.

In a unique way, Sally has that opportunity. As a member of the curriculum task force at her school, she will come in contact with Black and Hispanic parents and have an opportunity to get to know what they want for their children and why. I liked Sally's response to the parents and teachers at her meeting when the curriculum was questioned: "Look at what we have to work with." The question now is how do you replace it with something that respects both the teaching of necessary skills and the social and cultural relevance to these students as adolescents and as members of minority groups. I don't necessarily think an afrocentric curriculum will do that. Too much emphasis on "Africa over there" and the "slavery days" may not allow students to see their current role and image in society. But that doesn't mean it is not necessary to accurately depict the contribution of all ethnic groups in the curriculum. This goal is not incompatible with the need for rigor and the teaching of skills that would put these students on par with White suburban students although that is how it is presented in this case study: Either you are for it or against it.

The general lack of interest in the parents' concerns on the part of the teachers didn't surprise me. It also highlights the general low expectations some teachers have for students of color. I think Sally's dilemma is how to balance the desires of the parents with her status as a new teacher on the staff. She risks being ostracized by either group. Again, she will need the skills of being bicultural, only in this case it is not only in relationship to ethnicity, but also professional and social cultures (the culture of parents vs. the culture of teachers, which can be at odds sometimes).

In closing, I think the issue of social biculturalism on the part of White teachers working with large numbers of students of color is one that needs to be examined more closely in these case studies and in teacher education as a whole.

—Mother and Prospective Teacher

READER REACTIONS TO THE THREE CASE STUDIES

II

PUBLIC ARGUMENTS

Education in most democracies is a publicly funded, state-supported endeavor. Parents send their children to public schools with the expectation that they will be educated. Individuals are certified by states to teach in those schools. The curriculum, at least the formal curriculum, is frequently decided, or at least contested, in public forums. Public schools are *public* institutions and as such they are the focus of much discussion and analysis. These discussions occur in homes, in the local newspaper, at school board meetings, among elected officials, and at corporate headquarters. For too long a teacher's professional education has ignored these discussions. As we noted in the preface, teacher education has tended to limit professional preparation to a focus on the school site. This is unfortunate. Teachers need to understand the types of claims that are made about students, teachers, and the functions and purposes of education. They need to take part in, in fact we would say at times lead, those discussions. Today, there are teachers who do just that. Sadly, however, their professional education may not adequately prepare them for that role. We think it is time for teacher education to change.

In Part I we presented case studies so as to highlight various issues connected with the topic of culture and teaching. In Part II, we take those issues and respond to, interpret, and articulate them in three very different fashions. We have purposely tried to compose public arguments that represent existing views and we have tried to represent a broad spectrum. We have prepared "conservative," "radical," and "progressive" public arguments and have entitled them: "A Conservative View: Shared Cultural Visions—Shared Educational Bounty," "A Radical-Multicultural View:

Culture, Knowledge, and Transformation," and "A Progressive View: Culture, the Child and the Curriculum." In the conservative orientation we have underscored their emphasis on content knowledge and character education, and on schooling as a "cultural and social glue." In the radical orientation we have highlighted their emphasis on cultural differences, societal inequalities, culturally sensitive instruction, and curriculum. And in the progressive public argument we have underscored their desire to disentangle education and politics, balance the emphases on the curriculum and the child, and understand the child "on his or her own terms."

These views not only represent public arguments about culture, teaching, and schooling; they also capture features of our ways of looking at the issues. We hope that an examination and discussion of these public arguments will enable readers to make further sense of the claims heard and read daily, and help you to articulate and understand better your own views. We honestly doubt if any individual's views will fit easily into any one of these "slots." We are complicated beings. It is most likely that you will find that you share ideas and sentiments with two and probably all three of the public arguments. To that end we encourage you to "enter" into each point of view, understanding it on its own terms and to also look at each one with some distance and skepticism.

After each public argument we raise additional general and specific questions and issues. We do not elaborate a lengthy list but encourage you, especially in your class discussions and analyses, to explore these positions further. We do, however, link the public arguments to the case studies in Part I. We hope that linkage will enable a further discussion of the particular incidents in Part I and the general claims made in Part II.

A "CONSERVATIVE VIEW": SHARED CULTURAL VISIONS—SHARED EDUCATIONAL BOUNTY

Introduction

As U.S. citizens, we are the heirs of a prominent culture and a notable history. Unfortunately multicultural education proponents would have us doubt, even deny, this common legacy. This cannot continue. Our schools and their teachers must pass on this cultural legacy to all students. If teachers and schools do not emphasize our common heritage, we will fail both as a nation and as a people. If the voguish multicultural talk about differences, distinct cultures, and unique ethnic contributions overshadows our shared features we will crumble from within. Without a strong and resolute common identity we will be weak. For it is only with this sense of common identity that we can battle the divisive forces that threaten to tear us apart. As William Bennett (1992) argues, we desperately need a common culture, for

> [our common culture] is our civic glue. [It] serves as a kind of immunological system, destroying the values and attitudes promulgated by an adversary culture that can infect our body politic. Should our common culture begin to break down, should its fundamental premises fail to be transmitted to succeeding generations, then we will have reason to worry. One vital instrument for the transmission of the common culture is our educational system, and we need to ensure that our schools meet that responsibility. (p. 195)

We hear frequently, in loud grating tones, that Black, Hispanic, and other ethnic minority students have been mistreated. Supposedly they are the victims of an oppressive system. Not all students face the same obstacles and minority students certainly have not had it easy. But if we accept the view that portrays minority students as victims we will never win any of our future battles. In order to succeed in this life of ours (one that is becoming more intense, competitive, and fast-paced), all students must recognize their potential, must be given the knowledge to compete in this world, and must be shown the paths to do so. Acquiring this knowledge is not an easy task. These lessons cannot be learned by students who view themselves as victims and they cannot be taught by teachers who concern themselves mainly with their students' self-esteem. A positive and formidable sense of self can only be achieved through hard work, determination, and perseverance. In fact, those features constitute a central part of our national character. As a nation, we have examined the tough issues and persevered in difficult times. As a people, we have noted our failings and worked to overcome our weaknesses. All students should understand, be a part of, and embody this unique cultural heritage.

Our Common Culture

Our emphasis on shared culture is not fueled by a blind sense of patriotism. Our stress on common culture is motivated by a number of real concerns and informed by a number of important issues. We begin from the common and uncontroversial premise that in order to participate in a country's shared legacy its citizens have to understand what that legacy is all about. For example, if you want to participate in a democracy you need to know the history and the central features of that form of government. It is essential to understand our system of representation, the procedures for voicing one's concerns, the structures of our local and federal governments, and sources for further information. Without knowledge of the democratic structure there can be precious little civic participation.

But this principle is not confined to the civic or social studies curriculum. It is a principle that applies to the most basic features of our curriculum. For example, in order to read, in order to comprehend the text of a newspaper, one must understand the references and allusions to our fund of common cultural knowledge. All students need to have some passing acquaintance with the bits of knowledge that most Americans already know. If a passage in a text alludes to the Depression, Thomas Alva Edison, or the Emancipation Proclamation a student must understand those references in order to make sense of the text. Without this common body of knowledge students will not understand the literate world around them. Without an immersion in cultural literacy they cannot share in the common legacy that is uniquely and truly American. And without that common understanding they will not be able to participate in our shared way of life.

It has become fashionable (once again) to believe that learning must be "meaningful" and that the child must be "understood." Today's educational bureaucrats emphasize the distinctiveness of the cultural populations that attend our public schools and maintain that teachers need to understand the background and culture of each student. Such pronouncements are unrealistic and originate more from a sense of what is politically correct than what is educationally desirable. It is time to recognize that democratic participation in our society requires teachers to teach the basics, and to teach them in a fashion that will stick. Today's educators have forgotten that young children love memorizing nursery rhymes and enjoy singing repetitious verse. Such material forms the basis for a significant portion of a child's shared cultural knowledge. Numerous lessons can be gleaned from traditional rhymes and stories like "Jack and Jill" and "Hansel and Gretel." It is not an unforgivable imposition to have children read and recite these texts. What is unforgivable is for middle-class children to receive this sort of instruction at home while disadvantaged children are not exposed to it. All children should share this knowledge and it is the school's function to impart it.

Differences, Harms, and Wrongs

Rather than giving students the opportunity to study what binds us together, our multicultural critics emphasize the unique cultural contributions of each and every group. As a result, our differences, not our commonalities, are emphasized. We end up with little to celebrate and much to bemoan. We no longer see our triumphs but instead are continually shown our failures. If current sentiments prevail soon we will no longer honor the discovery of the Americas through celebrating Columbus Day. Native American protests have renamed it an era of massacre. What used to be known as the "Christmas break" has now become the "winter holiday"—so as not to offend the non-Christians among us. And now when we talk of families we have to include the extended family, the single parent, and those "parents" of the same gender. It seems that every imaginable "familial" permutation has to be mentioned and duly noted. And today, minority members refer to themselves as African Americans, Asian Americans, and Mexican Americans. Why can't we all be called Americans? We are in danger of losing any common sense of purpose or identity, and any shared sense of understanding.

Along with the calls to pay more attention to the cultural differences of each and every imaginable splinter group, we are served an endless platter of the harms and wrongs that have been inflicted on every group. Asian Americans were incarcerated during the war. African Americans continue to live under the legacy of American slavery. And Mexican Americans are not allowed to practice their native language in the schools. For every group there is a particular legacy but all (supposedly) share the legacy of exploitation. These groups have gone too far.

It is an aphorism among some educators that you talk about what you value. When little emphasis is given to the shared features of our democratic way of life, we can expect that it won't be valued for much longer. When we no longer value this way of life we will surely see our freedoms erode, and our way of life destroyed. It is not an alarmist message that we are sending, instead it is a realistic appraisal of the situation. As Bennett (1992) frankly states: "We are in the midst of a struggle over whose values will prevail in America" (p. 11). We are battling for the survival of our Western democratic culture and if we lose this battle we will certainly lose the war.

The Acclaimed Antidotes: Self-Esteem and the Multicultural Curriculum

According to many liberals, schools are supposed to remedy all of the wrongs and celebrate the noted differences through an enhanced focus on the child's self-esteem, an altered and culturally sensitive curriculum, and an understanding of the forces that harm these children—these victims. But this perspective misunderstands the nature of education and the processes of learning. Schools do not exist as institutionalized therapy sessions and learning should not focus solely on the learner's self-concept or self-image. Claims that minority members need to understand their cultural roots through learning more about their culture's contributions to our subject matter and knowledge base are misguided. And if one persistently views and treats minority children as victims of a larger system of oppression these students will never become empowered to act in constructive ways. Before we elaborate our preferred educational program, we explore more fully the three themes of self-esteem, a "multicultural" curriculum, and children as victims.

Self-Esteem.   In recent years we have witnessed an avalanche of educational programs and curricula designed to enhance the self-esteem of minority students. Educators want low-achieving minority students to feel good about themselves so that they can then learn and progress through school. The explanation and rationale for this situation is something like this: One of the major reasons why minority students do not do well in schools is because all of our "societal messages" inform them that they are inferior. In our society if you don't look like the average individual (White and middle class) you are made to feel inferior. Students who walk into the schools feeling inferior are hampered right from the start. With damaged self-esteem, they cannot attend to learning. The proposed solution is to help students feel better about themselves, which will motivate them to do better in school. Once they view themselves in a positive light they will be able to learn. Unfortunately, this view of the problem just makes the situation worse. We know from numerous studies that students can feel marvelously about their personal and academic strengths when in reality they fail abysmally at the academic tasks assigned. The key to enhanced minority achievement is neither a curriculum of self-esteem nor a curriculum of harms and wrongs. Instead, the key is a curriculum that challenges students to use their minds, disciplines their thinking, and rewards them for the work they have accomplished and the standards they have achieved. It is instruction that gives them the necessary skills and the opportunities to practice those skills. What is needed are teachers who set high expectations for their students and who persistently push and prod them to do their best. As Chester Finn (1990) claims, "the aspect of self-esteem which (some) minority students need more of is the type associated with bona-fide achievement, not the kind related to group pride" (p. 44).

"Multicultural" Curriculum.   In addition to the focus on self-esteem we have witnessed attempts to make the curriculum "multicultural." This means many different things to many different people—but a common

theme that resonates within this Tower of Babel is that in a diverse society the curriculum needs to "honor" that diversity. Some of the more extreme adherents of the multicultural orientation maintain that our existing curricular content is essentially "Eurocentric." Supposedly, such a curriculum enhances White people's self-esteem while harming all others. It enables the White majority to do well in school but creates obstacles for children of color. According to this critique, the history stories recounted in schools tell the story of White conquest and elitist progress: They diminish the pain and travails of the vanquished. The literature offered in schools rarely includes serious work by people of color and when such work is studied it is served as a palliative to quell those who might object. Even our mathematics and science curricula are said, by some, to ignore the contributions of people of color.

If we accept these multicultural versions then we will certainly, as Diane Ravitch (1991) notes, encourage

> the politicization of all curricula in the schools. If education bureaucrats bend to the political and ideological winds, … we can anticipate a generation of struggle over the content of the curriculum. … Demands for "culturally relevant" studies, for ethnostudies of all kinds, will open the classroom to unending battles over whose version is taught, who gets credit for what, and which ethno-interpretation is appropriate. (p. 351)

Multicultural proponents also ignore basic educational facts. No matter who influenced the development of mathematics, one must learn and memorize the basic facts of math. The sum of 2 + 2 does not change with cultural contexts. One can know that the Egyptians and the Mayans had developed sophisticated mathematical understandings but still do quite poorly in math. And simply including writers of color in the literature curriculum so as to have minority representation in the curriculum bespeaks the worst type of tokenism. Works in the high school English curriculum are there because they express and embody our shared cultural values: They are the great works. If one can locate authors of color that have achieved those heights then of course they should be included. But all too often multicultural sloganeers are enforcing a quota system; they are not enhancing our cultural understanding. Little substance is offered in the "multicultural" curriculum and, as a result, little educational progress will be achieved. One does not enhance students' educational achievement through pandering to their immediate interests or satisfying every vocal and local interest group. Educational progress is achieved only through diligence, effort, self-sacrifice, and plain, old fashioned, hard work.

Children as Victims.   One of the effects of this focus on self esteem and the push for a multicultural curriculum is the reinforcement of the view of the "minority student as a victim." In much of the multicultural literature—the world appears to be populated by two types of people: the oppressors and the oppressed—the dominant class and the victims. But victims are not active agents in this world view and as such they can take little part in improving their lot. Certainly, many minority groups have experienced hardships that others have not endured. And certainly even today some minority students face hardships that others do not have to confront. But when students begin to see themselves as victims they blame their entire situation on others—they claim that they are the victims of societal injustices. In doing so they shift the onus of responsibility onto others: They shoulder no blame and believe themselves to be innocent. With such a view of things, it is difficult to see how these students will act to improve their lot. Students who see themselves as victims are not the students who will achieve in schools.

And so it seems to us that much of the current focus on culture in schools serves little educational purpose. In fact it appears that many of the multicultural programs and proposals detract from rather than enhance students' educational progress. Next, we outline briefly what is required of all schools and of all students (regardless of color) so that everyone has a fair chance of school success.

Our Plan: Academics and Character for All

First of all schools and their students should aim at academic success. As a society, we currently are experiencing a number of difficulties but schools cannot solve all of them. Teachers are (or at least should be) equipped to do one job well and that task is the cognitive enhancement of all students. This is not to say that schools should not attend to the physical welfare of their students or note personal travails. Certainly a school needs to keep a watchful eye on students' physical and personal lives and, when appropriate, enhance their charges' physical and personal well-being. Teachers need to model healthy approaches to living and learning. And students must be engaged in activities that encourage their physical and personal well-being. But our schools' central task is an academic one—it is to ensure that all students master the required material so that they are informed, skilled individuals ready to make further life decisions.

Given that schools' central task is academic, how do we best achieve those academic goals? One common assumption is that we move directly to academic skills and curricular content. Certainly we need to focus on skills and content but we cannot forget that students' character, their moral fiber, will determine in large part whether they succeed or fail. Those who continually talk about the harms and wrongs inflicted on disadvantaged children treat them like victims. As we noted earlier, when students are treated like and begin to view themselves as victims, they become demoralized, self-preoccupied, and weak. Add to this demoralized state the fact that we live in an era that is "me-oriented" and thrives on instant gratification and even the smallest challenges look insurmountable to these students. Learning the necessary academic skills and content is not an easy task and these "victims" will neither survive nor thrive. All students need to develop the character that can enable them to stick it out even in the most difficult times. They must be able to persevere in the face of adversity, delay the desire for immediate gratification, be honest, respectful of authority, and punctual. Without character, students will be unable to learn, perform, and succeed.

Cognitive development and character betterment are the linchpins of our program and it is a program for all children. If we fail to give this sort of program to all of our children we will fail as a society, both politically and economically. And although we thus far have highlighted the political ramifications of this debate we have not yet mentioned the economic reverberations. We would be remiss if, before we closed our argument, we did not discuss the economic costs of the multicultural route.

We have borne the costs of the radical programs of the 1960s for much too long. What we see in today's inner city is the product of these programs. The decay, the blight, the crime, the fear, and the violence are products of programs that give handouts rather than challenge people to do their best. Now in those urban slums we see behavior that is simply unacceptable and costly. Children become parents and these parents do not work. Instead they play the deadly games of gratuitous violence, promiscuous sex, and illicit drugs. As a result of this behavioral poverty they are economically impoverished. This behavior harms them, those around them, and our society as a whole. The economic costs (not to mention the moral damage) are great.

This behavior has to be changed and it is only through an education that challenges their minds and uplifts their character that we will see improvement. We need schools that educate our future citizens to be productive and skilled members of the workforce. Other countries have outpaced our industrial growth. We must regain our international prominence as an economic giant. Skilled workers are needed and our schools can provide these workers.

These are difficult and heady times. Without a concerted effort on the part of teachers, students, and parents we will not successfully tackle these times. We need everyone's participation; we require everyone's effort. Only then will we become the nation that we once were and that we can truly become.

Comments and Questions

"The Conservative View and You"

General Questions

1. What aspects of this public argument seemed to capture your understanding of the school–culture debate?
2. What did you disagree with in this rendition?

Specific Questions

3. What comprises the "common culture" that conservatives propose?
4. Would a recognition of and value for cultural differences necessarily diminish a common American culture? If it would not, what would this common culture look like and what role would schools and teachers play?
5. Does the route to self-esteem offered by the conservatives, entail a denigration of some students' cultures? How so or why not?

Having read the conservative public argument, we think it helpful to revisit and reframe elements of the case studies presented in Part I. In the next few paragraphs we return to the case studies and utilize the conservative view to interpret and evaluate what happened.

"School and Home"

In Case 1: "School and Home," Anna spoke to Estella's parents about the options and choices for Estella's educational future. An explicit tension in this case study concerned the conflicts between the culture of schooling and the culture of the home. Anna went to Estella's house to outline the options at school. It seems that from a "conservative" point of view, Anna did the necessary thing but she could have and should have been both more forceful and confident in her approach. Schools offer the path of academic success and future reward. There was really no need for Anna to be so hesitant. When viewed from this conservative perspective how would you react to Anna's efforts and perceived dilemmas?

"Curriculum and Culture"

During the parent meeting at Rosa Parks High School, parents offered their perspectives on the existing curriculum and alternative curricular options. One group of parents wanted a more culturally sensitive curriculum, whereas another group called for a curriculum similar to the ones offered in "the suburbs." Both groups condemned the existing curricula as meaningless if not harmful. It seems that a conservative view would tend to agree with aspects of the critiques. However, they would view the call for a culturally sensitive curriculum as educationally useless. If a conservative editorial writer had reported and commented on this meeting what might he or she write?

"Teachers and Cultural Identities"

In a decidedly conservative voice, Rita Kramer (1991) critiques what she views as the simplistic and sad state of U.S. schools of education. In her book, *Ed School Follies,* she maintains that professors of education focus on fluff, not substance, and encourage an approach to education that emphasizes process rather than content. It seems that from the conservative point of view, Linda's professional preparation followed this simplistic and substanceless direction. The focus on teachers' and students' cultural identities along with the one professor's bilingual simulation exercise represent a politically correct but not educationally appropriate preparation. As a conservative student how would you react to Linda's teacher preparation program? From this perspective how would you appraise your own teacher education program?

A "RADICAL-MULTICULTURAL VIEW": CULTURE, KNOWLEDGE, AND TRANSFORMATION

Introduction

According to the more conservative members of our society, multicultural education encourages social decay and internal turmoil. We think the picture they paint is one that is far from reality and fueled by fear. They appear to be overwhelmed by the new demographics and fearful that they will soon find themselves the numerical minority in what was once *their* "democratic" society. Certainly, they are fearful of the changes to come. Try to alter the features of schooling that maintain their privilege, and they are quick to shout that such alterations will harm all children. Outline the harms that have been inflicted on children of color and they will tell you that such thinking only produces powerless victims. Attempt to right the wrongs of our checkered (and yes shared but not common) past, and they will tell you that our society is coming apart at the seams. The lesson from all of this is very clear but it is not the lesson that the conservatives want us to learn. Rather we think the lesson is this: Those who wield power do not like to yield it. They are certainly afraid and we believe they have reason to be.

For if we do not soon attend to the valuable differences that exist and make us the grand nation we are, and if we do not begin to understand all the forces that tear at us to weaken who we are, then we will live a life of fractured selves and become a defeated nation. It is only through a recognition of our differences and our shared humanity that we can move forward and claim what is rightfully ours. Our educational programs need to recognize, honor, and utilize these differences. And that means that within the United States power and leadership will have to be shared. A true democracy must be established. If not, our prominence as a people and a nation will weaken further, our sense of humanity will diminish even more, and our economic lives will be harmed.

Despite all the conservative rhetoric about our "shared" life and the importance of character and academics in our public schools, there are some facts that cannot be ignored. When we look at public school instruction, it is evident that cultural awareness and instructional practices are not mixing well together—they are like oil and water. Schools either ignore children of color or force them into molds that don't fit. But in order for good teaching to exist, teaching and culture have to inform one another. It seems so obvious. Teaching is communicating and any adequate communication must create meaningful interactions. Culture is the medium through which meaning and meaningful relationships are created. In order to teach well, cultural features have to be considered. Teaching, learning, and culture are inseparable. If teachers ignore the cultural heritage and knowledge of their students they will communicate poorly, the instruction will fail and so will the students.

It is time for each and every teacher to embrace these facts about teaching and culture. It is time for the curriculum to reflect the plurality that exists in our democratic society. Without a reflection of this plurality how can we really have a democracy? And it is time for our schools to empower those who have been disenfranchised. For when people are harmed, abused, discarded by a society, they do not disappear. They become the past legacies for a burdened future. Our teachers should act to dispel the lies and distortions that are contained within the curriculum, to include the omissions, and to right the injustices and harms that have been inflicted on people of color.

Some Essential Facts

When we, as multicultural individuals, raise our voices to protest the conditions of our children's schools we are told that progress has been made: It has come slowly, with determination and perseverance. But where are the signs of societal and educational progress? In the last decade, the gap between the rich and the poor has grown wider and wider. More and more "locked subdivisions" have appeared on the suburban landscape while the dislocated urban homeless population has increased. Throughout this country the plight of metropolitan school systems has become even more dismal. With a disappearing tax base the fiscal resources of our metropolitan schools have shrunk dramatically. Children of color are offered schools with fewer and usually dated texts, with teachers who appear at work but are resigned to do little teaching, and with facades and interiors that are ugly and crumbling. Multicultural education didn't make these buildings disintegrate. No, the problem lies with a racist society that will not honor the democratic principles of "freedom and justice for all."

Now certainly not all people of color are poor and we do not all live in the centers of large cities. But all too often poverty characterizes the lives of our brothers and sisters. For example, in Los Angeles the median household net worth in 1991 was $31,904 and for non-Anglos it was $1,353 (Leonard, 1993, p. 124). In our "City of Angels" it is obvious that too many people of color live a rather hellish existence. But not all people of color are poor. Within any minority population, there are vast differences. It is time that we see other people in all their distinctiveness. And it is time that we disabuse ourselves of the stereotypes that we have inherited. Sadly, however, one fact remains. A vastly disproportionate number of people of color live in poverty and attend schools that are grossly inferior to their White counterparts. We want that situation to change.

A Plan for Transformation: Culture, Curriculum, Instruction, and Teachers

What do we want? We want what all parents wish for their children: a safe environment in which they can learn about the world around them, develop pride and confidence in their abilities, and grow and enrich themselves through exploring and understanding the life that awaits them. What do we have to do in order to get these things? We have to alter the instruction, change the curriculum, and enlighten the teachers. The instruction must connect culture, the curriculum, and learning. The curriculum needs to reflect all children's unique and shared legacy, it must connect with their lives, and lead them to new challenges. And teachers must begin to recognize that these are necessary aspects of a multicultural education. Let's begin with those coming to the profession of teaching and then discuss further how both the curriculum and our instruction can become truly multicultural.

Teachers.   The majority of prospective teachers are White, female, and come from middle-class homes. In their lifetime they have had very little contact with other cultures or children of color. Most future teachers are well intentioned—that is, they enjoy children and want to help them learn. Unfortunately, their experiences are narrow and quite limited. Their understanding of culture and their knowledge of children of color is minimal. Their awareness of their own attitudes toward these children is just beginning to surface. And their ability to recognize and interact with other cultural patterns is restricted. In effect, these teachers are prisoners of their own experiences. Having had little experience with people and children from backgrounds different from their own, they have difficulty seeing our children clearly, with understanding and compassion. When these individuals become teachers they will have difficulty unlocking or altering the cultural barriers that confine children of color. They neither understand nor appreciate the magnitude of these barriers. A truly multicultural education would be led by teachers who understand children of color, who identify with their struggles and challenges, and who know the obstacles that lie ahead. They would be teachers who are sensitive to all children—who understand the nuances of language use, the patterns of students' daily lives, and the expectations that people hold. And, most importantly, they would be teachers who can teach. Our children desperately need the skills that public schools are supposed to impart.

Instruction.   Sound instruction is based on an understanding of the importance of cultural practices. If we view culture as the set of assumptions, understandings, and practices that help us understand and act on the world around us it becomes crucial for the teacher to see the child on the child's terms. There are plenty of studies that highlight the differences in children's behavior in and out of school. Hispanic students may speak English haltingly in school but be quite proficient as interpreters for their parents at home. African-American children may be quiet and shy in the classroom but curious and fully engaged in their own neighborhood. A teacher who understands that schools can affect children will not let the behavior they see in the classroom define the student. Schools can be strange places for some children and when anyone is in a strange place they tend to feel uncomfortable. When we're uncomfortable, we don't do our best. Good instruction begins from a comfortable, not a constrained, place.

Skilled instructors will also recognize that children bring different strengths and distinct dispositions with them to the school. Some Native American children do not like to be rushed to come up with an answer; they have been taught to take their time and to be deliberative. Some African-American children engage in an elaborate storytelling tradition, whereas teachers frequently expect their students to get to the point and be concise. All cultures have expectations and teachers need to be sensitive to the nuances of expression and meaning.

Children feel more comfortable when they see reflections of themselves portrayed in a good light. And although it would be best for children of color to have many teachers of their own cultural heritage, that probably won't happen for quite some time. Instead, we must settle for culturally sensitive teachers, sound instruction, and a curriculum that both centers on our students' experiences and reflects the plurality around them. For schools are cultural institutions that can embrace or reject the diversity of cultures that surround them. In order for people in a pluralistic society to engage in and become part of the democratic process, they need to see themselves reflected within that process—see themselves as part of the whole.

The Curriculum.   Why a "centered" curriculum? Molefi Keli Asante (1991–1992) talks about the importance of such a curriculum especially in an age that has left many children culturally homeless. In a telling passage, commenting on this reality for many African-American children, he states that:

> When it comes to facing the reality of social and cultural dislocation, teachers are on the front lines. They are among the first to see the devastation that has occurred to the African-American child's spirit. If they've been teaching for more than 20 years, they have seen more and more students who seem to have been dislocated culturally, socially, and psychologically. (p. 30)

Many children are growing up today without a sense of cultural location and psychological identity. Their communities and their schools have failed them. But these public schools have not failed White students as devastatingly as they have failed children of color. As Asante notes, "teaching is preeminently a communicating profession" (p. 29). Cultural similarity and shared understandings enhance communication. Asante continues:

> Most teachers do not have to think about using the White child's culture to empower the White child. The White child's language is the language of the classroom. Information that is being conveyed is "White" cultural information in most cases; indeed, the curriculum in most schools is a "White self-esteem curriculum." (p. 29)

White children receive a curriculum that "centers" them, whereas children of color do not.

All of our children need to be reconnected to the nuances and particular features of their inherited culture. They need to see and experience someone who has mastered their culture and engage in mastering it themselves. If they cannot experience this immersion they will not be centered and as a result they will be dislocated from their culture. Asante, focusing on the African-American child, is again helpful:

> African-American children who have never heard the Spirituals; never heard the names of African ethnic groups; never read Paul Laurence Dunbar, Langston Hughes, and Phillis Wheatley nor the stories of High John de Conqueror, Anansi, and the Signifying Monkey are severely injured in the most fragile parts of their psyches. Lacking reinforcement in their own historical experiences, they become psychologically crippled, hobbling along in the margins of the European experiences of most of the curriculum. (p. 29)

Our schools and their teachers must do better.

Culture and Language.   In many of our public schools, more than one cultural group is represented and so teachers need to become acquainted with their students' distinct cultures. Teachers are supposed to serve the communities in which they teach. If they are unfamiliar with those communities, part of their job is to learn about the needs, desires, and aspirations of the parents and children they serve. That may seem like an impossible task but it is not. It simply requires that teachers inquire, learn about, and become sensitive to the children whom they teach. If they already know about mainstream children, why should they not find out about other children? The alternative is not a desirable one. The alternative is forcing all of these children into a mold that does not fit and asking them to accept the death of their cultural identity. That seems like an extreme price to pay. Unfortunately, it is one that schools have exacted for many years and now must stop.

Every day children with language backgrounds other than English are forced to renounce their cultural connection and fit the White, Eurocentric mold. Part of the fabric of any culture is the language through which it is expressed. A student's connection to that culture and to her or his family, in fact their personal well-being and intellectual development, depends on using their native language. The best bilingual efforts are programs that encourage the use of both the home language and English and are built on the foundation of the student's native language. Good bilingual instruction recognizes that all children develop their underlying cognitive abilities through speaking in the language in which they are most proficient. Instruction in that language builds a strong foundation for proficiency and success in English. When bilingual programs become English submersion lessons, students are not allowed to utilize their developed talents. A good bilingual program will enable students to become truly bilingual and it will not do so at the cost of students' intellectual development and cultural connection. The culturally "dominant" tongue must be mastered; but it must not become the master.

But what frequently happens is just the opposite. The dominant language becomes the master and the linguistically diverse student may feel forced to face a choice that no one should have to confront: He or she must choose either to belong to his or her family and embrace its ways or renounce his or her cultural identity in order to succeed in mainstream society. In Richard Rodriguez's (1982) extended reflections on his life as a Hispanic and as a Rhodes scholar, he maintains that for the linguistically different student, academic achievement entails personal and cultural loss. According to Rodriguez, one cannot escape this fact. We don't believe it has to come down to this forced choice. But for many students, the deck seems stacked against them. If they choose to embrace their cultural identity rather than follow the path of mainstream success, they will be outcasts in educational institutions—academic losers; society then suffers as well. If they choose the academic route they become culturally dislocated.

But even portraying this dilemma as a choice is misleading. The choice is rarely articulated and frequently students find that the "decision" has been made for them. Schools structure the options and teachers "facilitate" the resolution. Teachers measure linguistically different students' academic promise through their assessed English ability. As a result, many students are judged to be in need of remedial attention. Schools have developed remedial routes for children whose native tongue is not English. Once students are placed in those settings little progress occurs. Unfortunately this story is one we hear all too frequently.

In a society that was truly multicultural students would not be forced to "choose" between academic success or cultural connection. Multicultural schools and teachers need to be sensitive to these dynamics and create bicultural avenues for all students.

There is a prevailing fear that bilingual education and a multicultural curriculum mark the sure and steady demise of a once great and remarkable nation. And there are those who claim that an emphasis on culturally distinct features diminishes the common, shared aspects of our lives. Nothing could be further from the truth. Within a multicultural, pluralistic nation an emphasis on differences and distinctiveness is natural. A recognition of the diversity is a strength that we should highlight and utilize. Such an emphasis does not obliterate our shared and essential humanity, rather it enhances it. We are all a complex, not simple, people and all of us want that recognized.

Some Final Thoughts

The problem today is that our mainstream society has ignored these differences, and they can be ignored no longer. When they are ignored or squashed they fester like an infected sore, becoming more irritated over time. In these situations, people become justifiably alienated. When any large segment of a society is alienated it is difficult for them to improve and enhance the society in which they live. It is the conditions that create this alienation that are corrosive to and divisive for our society.

Attempts to assert a "common curriculum" ignore the obvious. What has passed before as the common curriculum has not been common to us all. To be sure Emerson, Thoreau, and Shakespeare are important figures but we do not see reflections of ourselves in these White men. We do not see the legacy of exploitation and freedom denied in their works. We want the truth to be told—warts and all. We want to see the dreams of our nation studied and the nightmares examined. Our dreams will propel us into the future and our nightmares will remind us of our past mistakes. We want our students to examine democracy and diversity, slavery, and forced encampments. We should not shy away from either the beautiful or the ugly truths but rather examine our past with all its various manifestations, shades, and hues.

Before we close this discussion we need to address one final conservative claim. We frequently hear that "minorities are not the victims they portray themselves to be." And instead of "victim-talk," conservatives propose a "poverty" of behavior thesis. According to these conservatives poor people of color continue to live in poverty because they lack the skills and motivation necessary to succeed. They can neither delay gratification nor rise above their circumstances because they lack character. We will not excuse the violence and drug-induced rages that happen in our most blighted urban arenas. People everywhere must be responsible toward others. But what our conservative friends miss is the way in which many of our children are being set up for a life of frustration and anger. In a mass media society that is fueled by consumerism and profit, our children are daily exposed to vivid pictures of wants and desires forever deferred. They are shown what others have and by comparison their surroundings are worse than bleak, they seem unremittingly dismal. They are dismal because there doesn't seem a way out. No one is rushing into our cities to create jobs and factories. No one is setting a national policy that ensures a decent wage for a decent day's work. It seems that if you are born into poverty and then denied work—somehow you automatically lack character and are unable to delay gratification.

Education is certainly not the salvic response to this dismal and bleak situation. It seems difficult at times to find one's way past a racist, patriarchal, and capitalist society. But in the end, we must act and act in ways that affirm our own and others' humanity. In the end we must stand up and demand that the education we offer our children not be one that turns against them. It must be an uplifting and a courageous one. It must be an education that enlivens their souls, enables their minds, and empowers their bodies.

Comments and Questions

"The Radical-Multicultural View and You"

General Questions

1. What claims were made in this public argument with which you disagreed?
2. What features of this approach did you find commendable and worth pursuing?

Specific Questions

3. To what degree and to what extent can we expect schools and their teachers to change larger cultural and social dynamics?
4. Approached from this perspective, doesn't teaching become hopelessly complicated? Is there really any discernable way to factor culture into a teacher's instruction and curriculum?
5. Won't any centered curriculum exclude some? How can we have culturally centered and democratically focused schooling?

"School and Home"

Anna, in her efforts to talk to Estella's parents, recognized the tension between the culture of the home and the culture of the school. She did not make gross assumptions about Estella's family or her culture, but chose to make contact with them so as to discuss Estella's educational options. Anna, it seems, was moving in the right direction. But where was Anna's concern for Estella's Latina sisters—the ones who have not "shown" themselves to be so capable? What happens in Anna's classroom to make Estella shine above and beyond the others? From the radical-multicultural orientation it seems that Anna has much to understand and realize. What types of considerations and suggestions would you make to Anna?

"Curriculum and Culture"

Why is it when people of color disagree in a public setting they are either depicted as being "angry and mean" or it is noted that they did not seem "angry and mean"? In Case 2: "Curriculum and Culture," the one group of parents who called for a culturally appropriate curriculum were explicitly described as neither angry nor mean. Why is that? If you were one of those parents how would you describe that meeting to a friend and colleague? How would you react to the account as written in the text?

"Teachers and Cultural Identities"

It is about time that schools of education recognize that teachers carry into the schools sets of cultural assumptions that affect the education they will offer their students. Linda was lucky to have had those experiences but she still seems hesitant. She is neither committed to meaningful transformation nor objecting to it. But had her teacher education program been more personally transformative she might be experiencing fewer hesitations now. Had her teacher education program simulated life less and actually got her involved in real settings—then she might have grown to be more committed. Given the radical-multicultural orientation what types of experiences would you suggest be included in a transformative teacher education program?

A "PROGRESSIVE VIEW": CULTURE, THE CHILD, AND THE CURRICULUM

Introduction: Educational Plans not Rhetorical Ploys

In the culture–education debate, politics dominates. Conservatives, motivated by a fear of political chaos, announce that schools have to bind us together like a national glue. Supposedly, schools should inculcate in all students a shared culture and a common legacy. On the other side of the political spectrum, multicultural proponents, claiming societal injury and harm, maintain that schools need to affirm diversity and rectify societal injustices. People and cultures are distinct, and when teachers teach they need to take these distinctions into account. Purportedly, past injustices and present harms need to be examined and confronted. Unfortunately, both the conservatives and the multiculturalists are blinded by their ideological fervor. Schools' function is not to indoctrinate, mobilize, or enculturate but rather to educate. Only when we understand what it means to educate can we proceed through this thick and thorny debate.

Of course we must be realistic. Schools are publicly funded state institutions and as such they do have political functions. Parents want their children to learn general skills and to understand the world around them. Business interests want future workers who are capable, willing, and ready to work. But these expectations are general and reasonable. We can respond to these needs in an educative, not political, fashion.

But no matter how realistic these functions are, the heart of the educational enterprise is not political viability. No, the heart of the educational enterprise is the engagement of students' interests, the enhancement of their abilities, and the enlargement of their understanding of the world around them. Certainly a student's cultural background affects this educational enterprise. In order to enhance any student's abilities a teacher will need to communicate with that student. This communication is built on certain cultural assumptions. And so teachers need to be aware of the cultural assumptions that affect their communication. But there is a tendency to make much too much of all of this. There is a tendency to see the child as their cultural "markers" and not as the unique child that he or she really is. The child, as a special individual, is not addressed. When this occurs, cultural politics supplant educational responsibilities. Unfortunately, this happens all too often. It is probably one of the central tragedies of public education. Remarkably this travesty has persisted for more than a century.

The Child and the Curriculum

More than 90 years ago, John Dewey (1902/1956) stated that one of the central problems facing public education was its exclusive reliance on either the "child or the curriculum" to solve educational problems. According to Dewey, educational advocates either heralded the child or embraced the curriculum as the centerpiece of educational activity. Proponents of the child maintain that education must be adapted to the needs of the student, must facilitate the growth and development of the child, and must recognize the uniqueness of each individual. On the other hand, supporters of the curriculum argue that students need to know our established and stable body of knowledge, that this knowledge contains the summative fruits of mankind, and that without this knowledge students would have to reinvent the accomplishments of our inherited civilization.

In many ways, this century-old debate is still with us today. Today's conservatives focus on the importance of the curriculum, whereas the multiculturalists emphasize the child. Conservatives stress the adhesive force of the inherited curriculum. They maintain that all students must be initiated into the shared culture and knowledge that binds us together as a nation. On the other hand, the multiculturalists herald the "cultural" child as the most central element in the educational algorithm. The child and his or her culture become the focal point for the multiculturalists. Dewey argued then and we argue now that such a determined and singular focus harms, not helps, public education. In order to address our educational problems we need to bring together the concerns for the "child" and the "curriculum"; we need to see, as Dewey noted long ago, each as endpoints on the same line. We need to understand that our curriculum constitutes the accumulation of knowledge that represents solutions to past human problems, and that the child is actively engaged in solutions of his or her own problems. The use and creation of knowledge to solve problems constitutes the everyday reality of the child and the legacy of the human race. Once we see this clearly, a focus on either the child or the curriculum is insufficient. We cannot remain satisfied with either the conservative focus on the curriculum as our shared legacy or the multiculturalist emphasis on the "cultural" child. We must find ways to link the two together.

There is no one magical way or procedure that brings these two emphases together. Like any major educational decision it entails thoughtful deliberation and attention to the specifics of the situation. But for purposes of elaboration we can point to examples where education, not politics, is the focus, and where, as a result, students' lives are enhanced and enlarged.

Understanding Students on Their Own Terms

The hallmark of our more progressive approach is the belief that children are actively engaged in understanding the world around them. Students are neither passive recipients nor empty vessels. They inquire into, examine, and inspect their world. It is the teacher's task to figure out how children approach the world and to incorporate that understanding into their instruction. This needs to be underscored. All too often children, their interests, their beliefs, and their needs are left out of the educational equation. As a result the entire educational enterprise suffers. This cannot continue.

Eleanor Duckworth (1987) described the attempt of a number of teachers to comprehend children's understanding. She relates an incident involving two teachers who were asked to watch a videotape of two boys playing a game. The game involved one boy relating to a second boy the pattern and configuration of blocks that lay before him. The two boys were separated by an opaque screen, and the second boy had blocks in front of him but in no particular order. As the boys progressed, it soon became apparent that the boy who was to receive the instructions had "gone astray." In their initial viewing of the video, the teachers noted that there seemed to be a "communication problem" between the boys, that the boy giving the instructions had "well-developed" verbal skills, whereas the boy receiving the instructions had been "unable to follow directions." Then one of the researchers pointed out that she had heard the first boy tell the second one to pick up a green square (none of the squares were green—all squares were orange and all green blocks were triangles). When the teachers viewed the videotape again, they were amazed. They now saw that one minor mistake had set off all the resulting confusion. The teachers no longer saw the second boy receiving instructions as inept or unable to follow directions. Where previously they had perceived the boy as unable to follow directions, they now were able to discern the reasons for the boy's errors. The teachers came to understand better the reasons for the child's actions. Commenting on this instance Duckworth (1987) writes:

> One teacher said of [the researcher's] remark, "She gave him reason." She referred, of course, to the second boy, the pattern builder, to whom [the researcher] had been able to "give reason"—reason for behavior that had previously been seen merely as inattentiveness or perhaps inability to follow instructions. To "give a child reason" became the motto, the aim, of much of the teachers' subsequent work. This was the challenge they put to themselves every time a child did or said something whose meaning was not immediately obvious. That is, the teachers sought to understand the way in which what a child says or does could be construed to make sense—they sought to give him reason. (pp. 86–87)

As progressive educators we attend to students' understandings and build on them. Certainly there is a great deal of diversity in students' understanding, and as educators we need to attend to that diverse range.

Vivian Gussin Paley (1989) illuminates further the kind of approach that embodies an educative, rather than political, grasp of the situation. The author of many books and a practicing early childhood educator, Paley tells the story of her reactions to ethnicity and culture as a teacher. In her book, *White Teacher,* Paley notes that when she first started teaching she and her fellow White teachers "showed respect by completely ignoring Black people as Black people. Color blindness was the essence of the creed" (p. 9). But the denial of differences didn't seem to take Paley very far; her understanding and knowledge of her students was drastically curtailed. The denial of differences obscured the need for knowledge of how her Black children's cultural backgrounds might be quite different from those of some of her White children. This cultural knowledge, she argues, is an essential part of the educational picture. In *White Teacher,* Paley recounts a number of incidences in which further knowledge of the cultural context enriched her understanding of the situation immensely, especially with African-American children. But toward the end of the book she relates an experience with a fellow teacher that alters her perceptions once more.

One of Paley's fellow teachers, Sonia, objected to her characterization of a group of girls as the "Black girls." She argued that seeing these girls as "Black" obscured a number of telling features of each of the girls. And Paley (1989) states:

> Sonia was right. I had begun by looking at differences and slipped back into the cliches that obscure differences. "White girls" did not slip easily off my tongue as did "Black girls." I saw White children as individuals. If I used the group label "White" it was to round off a generalization made about Blacks. (p. 136)

Paley relates that she never engages in gross descriptions of "boys and girls" and that she shudders when she, as a Jew, hears others make generalizations about Jews. She then recalls the comments of one of her parents:

> Mrs. Hawkins, way back in my first year at the new school, had startled me when she said "My children are Black. They don't look like your children. They know they're Black and we want it recognized. It's a positive difference, an interesting difference, and a comfortable natural difference. At least it could be so, if you teachers learned to value differences more. What you value you talk about." Mrs. Hawkins never intended that these differences be used to lump children together and dim the uniqueness of each child. But she knew that these differences must be treasured by the Black child and the White teacher. (p. 138)

Differences and diversity have to be valued.

But frequently too much of a political interpretation is given to these differences—to diversity. The conservatives fear it as politically divisive and the multiculturalists see it as a political mandate. We believe that in all of this ideological banner waving the child becomes lost. Diversity is an essential feature of all living creatures—it is essential for the perpetuation of human and other species. It is a biological fact. But all too often the diversity among any group of students, even a group of "homogeneous" White, middle-class children is overlooked. Unfortunately, many people also view all "poor" African-American children as similar. Hispanic children are frequently lumped together. But such views ignore the reality of life.

Vito Perrone (1989), the former dean of the New School and Center for Teaching and Learning at the University of North Dakota and currently professor of education at Harvard, made a telling point some 20 years ago. In an address to the Association for Childhood and Education International entitled "The World's Children: Valuing Diversity," he made the following statement, one that deserves to be reprinted in its entirety:

> Valuing diversity in our schools calls for beginning with the child—acting on the assumptions that learning is a personal matter, varies for different children, proceeds best when children are actively engaged in their own learning, takes place in a variety of environments in and out of school, and is enhanced in a supportive setting where children are taken seriously. To act on these assumptions would mean challenging the ways most teachers, schools, and classrooms now function. Normative orientations, which include predetermined expectations for children at prescribed ages would, for example, begin to collapse as would most standardized testing. A diversity of options for learning would be available. As most teachers have come to understand, the opportunities for successful experience and increasing levels of self-esteem are related to the range of options available to children. (p. 6)

It seems that we need to cultivate a thousand flowers and let them bloom. We need to understand each of those "blooms" and then engage them in their own learning.

Making Connections To and Within the Curriculum

But thus far we have focused mainly on the child "side" of the child and curriculum connection. Now we need to highlight the curricular side. In Dewey's famous restatement of the child and the curriculum conundrum, he noted that all too often we bring knowledge to the classroom that is ready-made, finished, completed, and packaged. Any connection to the real problems that animated its discovery is lost. He speaks of the early maps of the western frontier as end products of adventurous exploring and problem solving. They represent the accumulated experiences and explorations of different individuals. In schools, we figuratively and literally give to students finished maps. Dewey called for this to end almost 100 years ago; today we echo, affirm, and reinforce that call. We should offer students experiences that convey the problems and the solutions that went into the creation of all of our "maps"—all of our fixed bodies of knowledge. When students are fed ready made problems and solutions, they are not engaged in their learning. When they are lectured at and informed about subject matter, subject matter whose purpose is hidden and contained, there is no reason for them to become engaged.

The conservative's curriculum talks at students, it does not engage them. Having students memorize nursery rhymes so that they can become culturally literate is instructionally weak and ill-conceived. Lecturing students about the structure of cells, the parts of speech, and the structure of our governing bodies misses the mark. Certainly, learning centered around perennial children's rhymes can be pleasant and engaging if it is handled appropriately and carried out for the right purposes. But the conservatives want children to become schooled, not engaged, with some larger cultural understanding. They want to impose not to educate. They want to feed the child ready-made inert subject matter that has little life and little spark for children. They say they want children to become a part of and to understand their shared culture but it seems they do damage to both the understanding and the shared features of any potential culture. Children schooled under the conservative's curriculum would neither share nor value the much heralded "common" culture.

Conclusion

When the student becomes an engaged child, and when the curriculum becomes the material through which students actively understand the world around them, the diversity and distinctiveness that surrounds us will come alive. When we force either a ready-made curriculum formula or talk only about a student's own culture, we do not educate. And we must educate if we are to progress.

Comments and Question

"The Progressive View and You"

General Questions

1. What aspects of the progressive view did you find to be agreeable?

2. What elements did you sense were either unrealistic or out of tune with the current realities of schooling?

Specific Questions

3. Progressives claim that their orientation takes "politics" out of educational plans. At the heart of the progressive educational enterprise is an enlargement of students' understanding of the world around them. How can that not be political? If we engage students in understanding the social and political institutions around them, aren't we asking them to look at power relations and to come to terms with those power relations?
4. Progressives claim that they alone attempt to balance culture, the child, and the curriculum. Don't the conservatives and the radicals do that also, but only on their own terms?
5. Progressives speak of student engagement and excitement. Are they missing the difficulties, challenges, headaches, and tiresome features of learning? Are they trying to sell us an unrealistic orientation?

"School and Home"

If more teachers followed Anna's lead we would find a greater proportion of students of color engaged in school. Anna's efforts represent an attempt to offer choices to students and their families and to involve them in educational decisions. But Estella seems oddly present and yet strangely absent. Why didn't Anna talk with Estella about these issues? What does Estella think about all of this? What does Anna do in the classroom to engage Estella and other students with the curriculum? In what ways has Anna changed or altered the curriculum to address the needs and concerns of her students? These seem to be some of the questions and issues that a progressive educator would underscore. What others should be raised?

"Curriculum and Culture"

Even though the parents and some of the Rosa Park High School staff met and discussed the school's curriculum and instruction, they have a long way to go. The two parent groups seemed to voice the curricular options most frequently delineated. Either we emphasize the cultural child or we underscore the subjects of study. Why is it that we persist in framing our educational choices in an either–or fashion? Let's assume that Sally has a true progressive "soul"—what approach should she take at her next meeting to move the school in a progressive direction?

"Teachers and Cultural Identities"

Linda has been educated to be sensitive to her students' needs. Her emphasis on home visits and her awareness of the role language and culture play in schools are essential features for an enlightened approach to education. But it seems that Linda may end up erring on the side of the cultural child—and forget the need to integrate the child and the curriculum. What does Linda want to teach her students? How will she enable them to explore actively the world around them? What knowledge will her students need? These are essential questions that Linda seems to overlook.

III

A FINAL ARGUMENT, AND SOME SUGGESTIONS AND RESOURCES FOR FURTHER REFLECTION

In this final section we accomplish three distinct tasks. We present briefly the main elements of our own considered public argument; we outline some exercises, activities, and questions that should encourage a further reflection over the issues raised thus far; and finally we present a list of books and articles that are good resources for further reading and discussion. In Part II we indicated that many teachers find valuable features in all three of the public arguments. Many of us carry around views about schooling and teaching that are more eclectic than the "typical" or "standard" views. We know we do. And we also root ourselves in a particular orientation—what we have called the radical or social reconstructionist perspective. That is, we have as one of our prime concerns the manner in which larger social and cultural dynamics affect, and in the process often harm and distort, the education we offer to many of our students of color. We are centrally concerned with the manner in which we can create educational settings that recognize both the shared and distinct understandings of peoples from varied backgrounds. There are two basic reasons for articulating our views. Since we put this text together we thought we owed you a more formal presentation of our perspectives and assumptions. This is not an assumption-less text. But at the same time, we have tried not to create a work that would point you in a particular direction, or bias you in a particular fashion. Instead, we hope this work encourages you and others to raise crucial issues and reflect on them. We think it is important that you are at least aware of our biases and assumptions. You should know where authors—all authors—stand. We also think it is important to offer an example of a reaction, or a public argument, that is a bit more eclectic. Although the radical view comes pretty close to our own, we emphasize elements that draw from other public arguments. Because we believe it is important for you to begin to articulate your own views and assumptions, we offer our own understandings as one way to put together views on the issues of culture and teaching.

In the first volume of this series, *Reflective Teaching*, we highlighted the active and reflective role of the prospective and practicing teacher. Another way to think further about the issues outlined in this text is to inquire, both formally and informally, into the world around us. We think classroom observations, letters to editors, attendance at school board meetings, visits to social service agencies, home visits, and textbook analyses are crucial activities and learning experiences. We outline some of these in hopes that you will be encouraged to try some, inquire, and reflect further.

Finally, we list the books, pamphlets, and articles to which we have referred in this text and others that we have found useful. Most of these should be available at your college or university library or at another nearby library. Most libraries have an interlibrary loan process available—and we would encourage you to utilize that service.

CULTURE, TEACHING, AND SCHOOLS: AN ABBREVIATED VIEW

What to Do?

The issues raised by the intermingling of culture, teaching, and schooling seem to lack any simple or easy resolution. Numerous questions come to mind and include: How does one create more equitable and just educational settings in a society that is essentially inequitable and unjust? How does one utilize the dynamics of culture when those dynamics seem to put students of color at a disadvantage? and Should all students experience some common core of subject matter or are we left with a situation that is much too divided and divisive for that? Realistically, the solutions are not simple, the obstacles are many, and the promising possibilities few. If one examines the historical record of public schooling, or the sociological and anthropological research on schools, the pictures are not at all rosy. In fact, they are rather bleak. We are not a society that has provided poor students or students of color with access to our public resources and common knowledge. In fact we are not a society that devotes much of our substantial resources to our students or children. Our society is class-based, racially divided, and essentially masculinist in its orientation. Greed and consumerism are at its core. The accumulation of wealth and status are its motivating forces. During our more dismal days, it seems that any progress that we are likely to make will be progress that will be taken away. Looking at the big picture, examining the structure of our society, it all can seem foreboding and quite discouraging.

We cannot lose sight of this admittedly dismal picture. And we cannot lull ourselves into thinking that we can alter long established societal patterns. However, if we are educators, and if we are going to engage in education, then we must have hope. We must understand that lives and institutional patterns can be changed and we must find ways to enact our hope for and in students. In the past few years we have come to believe that teaching without hope is a losing proposition, a no win situation for everyone involved. Minimally, it seems, that education is about learning and learning entails change and alteration in, and transformation of the learner. If we have learned we have changed in some minimal or significant way. And so when we educate we must do so with hope, with the hope that our efforts are meaningful and valuable to the people with whom we interact. That much is plain and that we accept. However, in our own lives we no longer sustain the belief, the hope, that our educational efforts will be the driving force in the creation of a more equitable and just society. They may contribute to the creation of a better world; that much we acknowledge. But we no longer hold the hope for societal transformation as our sustaining belief and goal guiding our educational work. We certainly hope, and will work to ensure, that our actions will affect students and others in meaningful ways. But we have come to realize that education is not the place for adults to expect the kind of societal change that arises from mass movements. For adults, the streets and their cities, their neighborhoods, homes, and workplaces are sites for the type of significant political and social transformation that is rooted in class-based and grass roots organized efforts. Not all significant change must have foreseeable structural effects. For children significant action and transformation is occasioned through an education that enlivens their minds, bodies, and spirits. In schools we must do what we can, we must make every effort possible, to offer students an education that is meaningful and empowering.

Education affects individuals, and when "added together" our educational efforts can contribute and have an affect on the larger society. But to invest our transformative political and societal hopes in schools and children is to misplace our expectations. It is to lose sight of the real nature of the problems—to ignore the fact that some of problems are much more deeply rooted, that they may constitute features of ourselves and our society that too many people are simply not prepared to recognize. And if the problems are recognized they may entail changes that too many are unwilling or unable to accomplish. Transforming the daily lived practices and beliefs that undergird capitalism, patriarchy, and racism are tasks of a rather large order. This we have to recognize. But in the face of all of this we are not resigned and we do not give up. No, it seems as teachers we must act, we must have hope, and that as a result of those actions we will be affirming both our students and our beliefs. We hope that we will have a positive impact on students and in some way on the world in which they will live. But we admit that we really don't know what the impact might be.

The Permanence of Racism and the Necessity for Action

We find many of these and similar sentiments expressed quite well in a book by Derrick Bell (1992) entitled, *Faces at the Bottom of the Well.* In this collection of essays and short "stories" Bell, a Black legal scholar, maintains that racism is in all likelihood a permanent feature of our society, one that cannot be eradicated and one with which we must come to terms. For Bell and others (e.g., Andrew Hacker, in his *Two Nations: Black and White, Separate, Hostile and Unequal*, 1992), we live in a society in which Whites define themselves by who they are not: They are not Black or people of color. This definition, this exclusion of others, is a psychological basis for racism, it is a sort of "White bonding." Focusing on the intersection of poverty and the issue of race Bell (1992) explains:

> Whites, rather than acknowledge the similarity of their disadvantage, particularly when compared with that of the better-off Whites, are easily detoured into protecting their sense of entitlement vis-à-vis Blacks for things of value. Evidently, this racial preference expectation is hypnotic.
>
> … Whites are rallied on the basis of racial pride and patriotism to accept their often lowly lot in life, and encouraged to vent their frustration by opposing any serious advancement by Blacks. Crucial to this situation is the unstated understanding by the mass of Whites that they will accept large disparities in economic opportunity in respect to other Whites as long as they have a priority over Blacks and other people of color for access to the few opportunities available. (pp. 7, 9)

Bell believes that a significant amount of "racial bonding" by Whites has and probably will occur. For people of color this means that their "rights and interests are always vulnerable to diminishment if not to outright destruction" (p. 9). Given our history and the legacy of a persistent racial bonding among most Whites, Bell asks us to consider and accept the following proposition:

> Black people will never gain full equality in this country. Even those herculean efforts we hail as successful will produce no more than temporary "peaks of progress," short-lived victories that slide into irrelevance as racial patterns adapt in ways that maintain White dominance. This is a hard-to-accept fact that all history verifies. We must acknowledge it, not as a sign of submission, but as an act of ultimate defiance. (p. 12)

Many react to Bell's propositions with despair and resignation. Neither he nor we think that is the only or the most advantageous response. In fact, Bell outlines an alternative reaction. And in his alternative tact the search for meaningfulness is central. Bell admits that the work that went into the civil rights efforts was work that people accomplished with the hopes of success. But he thinks success was not the central motivating force. Instead, he views these emancipatory efforts as driven by a desire for meaningfulness. And meaningfulness, Bell writes, is a "by-product of engagement and commitment":

> This engagement and commitment is what Black people have had to do since slavery: making something out of nothing. ... Beating the odds while firmly believing in, knowing as only they could know, the fact that all those odds are stacked against them. (p. 198)

He also adds that:

> Both engagement and commitment connote service. And genuine service requires humility. We must first recognize and acknowledge (at least to ourselves) that our actions are not likely to lead to transcendent change and may indeed, despite our best efforts, be of more help to the system we despise than to the victims of that system whom we are trying to help. Then, and only then, can that realization and the dedication based on it lead to policy positions and campaigns that are less likely to worsen conditions for those we are trying to help and more likely to remind the powers that be that out there are persons like us who are not only not on their side but determined to stand in their way ... it is not a matter of choosing between the pragmatic recognition that racism is permanent no matter what we do, or an idealism based on the long-held dream of attaining a society free of racism. Rather, it is a question of *both, and. Both* the recognition of the futility of action—where action is more civil rights strategies destined to fail—*and* the

unalterable conviction that something must be done, that action must be
taken. (pp. 198–199)

Bell does not speak of hope. In fact some read his work as undermining a
sense of hope. We do not. It seems he is asking us to recognize that our
actions do not always produce the outcomes we desire but not to let that
recognition diminish our resolve to act. As educators, it is apparent to us
that not all of our educational efforts produce the effects we desire and it
would be counterproductive to let that recognition curtail our work. Realism
and hope are both necessary.

Others are more explicit in how they underscore the need for a sustaining
and nurturing hope. Both Cornel West (1993) and bell hooks (1994) speak
of combating racism and White supremacy with an attitude of love. In
answering the question, "Is there really any hope, given our shattered civil
society, market driven corporate enterprises, and White supremacism?"
West writes that the chance for transformation rests

neither on an agreement about what justice consists of nor on an analysis of
how racism, sexism, or class subordination operate. Such arguments and
analyses are indispensable. But a politics of conversion requires more.
Nihilism is not overcome by arguments or analyses; it is tamed by love and
care. Any disease of the soul must be conquered by a turning of one's soul.
This turning is done through one's own affirmation of one's worth—an
affirmation fueled by the concern of others. A love ethic must be at the center
of a politics of conversion. (pp. 18–19)

And hooks reinforces this claim when she writes:

The absence of a sustained focus on love in progressive circles arises from a
collective failure to acknowledge the needs of the spirit and an overdeter-
mined emphasis on material concerns. Without love, our efforts to liberate
ourselves and our world community from oppression and exploitation are
doomed. As long as we refuse to address fully the place of love in struggles
for liberation we will not be able to create a culture of conversion where there
is a mass turning away from an ethic of domination. (p. 243)

West and hooks underscore the need for an ethic of care and compassion,
of love, in an age that is divided and strained. Bell highlights the role of
engagement and commitment. Teachers and teaching require all of this.

Our Educational Strategies

How does all of this affect our thoughts and plans about culture, teaching,
and schooling? We are not altogether sure, but we have embraced a few

basic beliefs. We are certain that teachers' and students' cultural assumptions affect the teaching and learning that occurs in schools. Therefore, we feel secure in maintaining that teachers need to attend to their own and their students' cultural identities and assumptions. Now this is not to say that a student or a teacher is her or his culture. And certainly White, Black, and Hispanic cultures are not single, monolithic, coherent cultural webs. Black, White, and Hispanic students should not be seen solely as White, Black, or Hispanic students. But a sensitivity to the cultural assumptions that surround schools and the cultural baggage that we all carry into schools should be, we think, an essential feature of schooling and teaching.

We still affirm the claim that "knowledge is power"—and recognize that our society and schools have disempowered many. Although we do not call for schools, teachers, and students to transform society, we think that an education for critical consciousness is crucial. That is, students should become aware of the ways in which we have not and do not live up to our democratic promise. Public education should not cover up our past transgressions and it should not offer lies about our present situation. This does not mean that second graders are introduced to content that depicts our past or present lives in gross or cynical terms. An education for critical consciousness needs to be sensitive to the many ways the human spirit can become twisted, cynical, and distorted. It needs to be sensitive to individual students and be "age appropriate." But an education for critical consciousness must also recognize that certain skills are needed by every "educated" adult in our society. All children need to be literate. All children need to have the skills that an information age requires. And an education for critical consciousness must be guided by and encourage in students a moral sensitivity—one that is concerned about justice, care, and the nurturance of the human spirit.

This last point requires elaboration. Schools and teachers can "build character." They sustain and encourage it through honest, caring, and nurturing interpersonal interactions and through the creation of classrooms that affirm each student. None of us has any exclusive purchase on how we can encourage our youth to become individuals of integrity, individuals who care for and share with others. But it seems certain that such an education entails simple old-fashioned modeling. Students need to see examples of adults before them who care deeply and act carefully in the schools and the surrounding neighborhoods. They need to hear adults voice their concerns and affirm their beliefs in others. Students need to see adults who make mistakes, acknowledge them, and then move on. Teachers must live a life that cares for and sustains others: Teachers need to be the kind of individuals that they want their students to become. These points are underscored and reinforced by Deborah Meier (1995) in her work at the Central Park East Secondary Schools in Manhattan, New York. As an educator working for meaningful and powerful education for all children she writes that:

> Caring and compassion are not soft, mushy goals. They are part of the hard core of subjects we are responsible for teaching. Informed and skillful care is learned. Caring is as much cognitive as affective. The capacity to see the world as others might is central to unsentimental compassion and at the root of both intellectual skepticism and empathy. "Any human being sufficiently motivated can fully possess another culture, no matter how 'alien' it may appear to be," argues noted African-American author and literary critic Henry Louis Gates. "But there is no tolerance without respect—and no respect without knowledge." Such empathetic qualities are precisely the habits of mind that require deliberate cultivation—that is, schooling. If such habits are central to democratic life, our schools must become places that cultivate, consciously and rigorously, these moral and intellectual fundamentals. (p. 63)

Beyond these broad sentiments there are more particular issues and concerns. Should schools in all Black neighborhoods offer an Afrocentric curriculum? In schools where the population is culturally heterogeneous how do teachers deal with the plurality of cultures? Is there such a thing as a common core curriculum for all students, and if so what should it look like? There are certainly many other issues but we address these three because they highlight crucial concerns and it is through a discussion of these issues that we can articulate further features of our approach.

Many White and Black middle-class individuals react to Molefi Asante's Afrocentric curriculum with horror and fear. They see in Asante's proposals a validation of a Black-African identity and a deemphasis on shared democratic values. They see a separatist orientation that is fueled by anger and resentment. We see in the Afrocentric movement a recognition of the pervasiveness of cultural values that diminish and demean young Black children's participation in schools. Such experiences are common, everyday occurrences. It is as simple as teachers posing questions that do not make sense to the students. Shirley Brice Heath (1982, 1983) captures this quite well when she documents how White middle-class teachers' use of instructional questions—What is this? (pointing to a pencil)—may seem very confusing to some students. (For the student it seemed odd for the teacher to ask about something so obvious. In fact, one Black child in Heath's study wanted to know why the teacher asked about things being themselves; Heath, 1982.) Students not used to this middle-class parenting style, one that is used frequently in early education, may seem confused and distant. Schools and teachers need to recognize the meanings that students bring with them to school and the type of environment that would support a powerful and empowering education. We certainly would not endorse a school program that is antidemocratic and we don't think culturally centric approaches need be separatist or antidemocratic. These approaches emphasize the importance of culture, of understanding where a child "comes from." This sort of emphasis need not be exclusionary. If parents and school staff want to pursue a centric route we think they should explore it, ensuring that it is neither repressive nor discriminatory toward others.

When teachers face students from many cultural backgrounds the task becomes more complicated but not, we think, impossible. Certainly there are limits to what we can know and experience. When teachers face a diverse classroom or five diverse sections it is unreasonable to expect them to be thoroughly multicultural. But if teachers have a bicultural understanding, recognize that assumptions matter and that our culture affects those assumptions, then they have a sensitivity that should profit both the students and themselves. With this sort of sensitivity teachers can recognize that they may not have the entire picture in front of them and that more information is necessary.

All of this attention to the nuances of multicultural difference need not diminish the need to highlight a core set of common understandings and experiences. Certainly a democratic nation needs to prepare its citizens for participation in that society. That preparation should emphasize content, knowledge, modes of inquiry, and forms of judgment. Although we certainly would not support an amalgamation of culturally approved bits of information along the lines of Hirsch's (1988) sanctioned list, we do think that something akin to Ted Sizer's (1992) approach or Deborah Meier's (1995) curricular orientation is potentially powerful. Sizer's emphasis on the content areas of mathematics and science, history and philosophy, and the arts (along with an emphasis on modes of inquiry and expression) would focus us further on what we should share. Meier highlights the central questions that her students and teachers have pursued, what she has come to call "habits of mind," indicating that they constitute the heart of her secondary curriculum. She writes that they are:

> the question of evidence, or "How do we know what we know?"; the question of viewpoint in all its multiplicity, or "Who's speaking?; the search for connections and patterns, or "What causes what?"; supposition, or "How might things have been different?; and finally, why any of it matters, or "Who cares?" (p. 50)

Sizer's and Meier's approaches emphasize an interdisciplinary approach in secondary education. Others would want to emphasize a less integrative endeavor. But that we should share a broad democratic orientation to the world is not in doubt. Working out the features of that orientation seems to be an ongoing process and something to which we as teachers and citizens should give more attention. It is time now to do just that.

When schools and their students are torn asunder by larger social forces, the schools and their students cannot mend the situation by themselves. Although we are not overly sanguine about the transformative role of public education, we do think that there are extremely important tasks to accomplish. Unfortunately, we may need to focus on what we can offer our students as antidotes to these larger social forces. At this time it may be as much as we can do and it may be a very powerful force in their lives and in the lives around them.

EXERCISES FOR FURTHER REFLECTION

Thus far, we have utilized either case studies or written public arguments as the basis for our reflections. We designed the case studies and the public arguments in ways that, we hoped, would encourage you to think both about educational policy and classroom actions, and your own beliefs and past experiences. In this final section, we felt that it would be helpful to suggest additional experiences, something distinct from a written text (see the abbreviated list offered in the Bibliography), that might facilitate further reflection on culture and teaching. In the paragraphs that follow, we have tried to offer, in as succinct and direct a fashion as possible, suggestions for other experiences that might provide more substance for thought and reflection.

Recommendations

Before we outline some of these experiences, a few recommendations are in order. It is not unusual for those first encountering the teaching profession and those who have been used to traveling their own path, to view particular experiences, to see classrooms and certain teachers, to look at children and the contexts from which they come, and in all of these situations to react and judge from an immediate appraisal of what they think is going on. It is difficult to look at a classroom interaction or an interaction that impinges on a student's schooling and not to interpret the scene or setting. But it is just that interpretation, or more accurately it is just those scenes along with the interpretations, that we want to construe as the stuff of reflection. Although we are not going to suggest that you observe without having reactions, we do want to recommend that you find ways to make your observations and to note your reactions. We have found again and again that good teaching is built on a reflective awareness of how, as teachers, our interpretations can facilitate or obstruct the teaching act. In understanding schools, students, and the communities in which schooling occurs, we need to be aware of the fact that other interpretations for the scenes we observe and the experiences we encounter exist. A prime example of this sort of thing was highlighted in the progressive public argument (see section on "A Progressive View—Culture, the Child, and the Curriculum) when Duckworth noted how teachers observed two students' interactions very differently after clarifying their understanding of the actual interaction. Events and experiences don't come ready made with interpretations—we bring ourselves and create the reactions and the interpretations. It is helpful, in fact it is necessary, to learn how to disentangle our interpretations from the scenes we observe and the experiences we have. In our own work observing student teachers we have found it very helpful to try to jot down notes, descriptions of actual interactions, and when we have noticeable personal reactions or interpretations to note those separately. What is key here is that we try to be aware of our judgments and reactions, attempt to separate those interpretations from the events and experiences, and to try to achieve a bit more distanced or "neutral" rendering of the events. So we want to suggest that when you engage in the experiences or observations outlined here, it will be important that you recognize and listen to your reactions, disentangle those reactions from your description of the "events," and then reflect on both your reactions and the events.

We happen to think that observations and experiences are best if they come from more integrated and less superficial interactions. For the school experiences we suggest ones that can, for the most part, arise out of your general practicum time in schools. For experiences in other types of institutions and settings we recommend that you offer to those involved some of your time and labor. We aren't suggesting a month's worth of work, but rather 12 to 16 hours of time. So as not to become a mere traveler through someone else's place and space, we hope that you can spend some time attempting to understand people and settings very different from your own.

Visit a Homeless Shelter.   Visit a homeless shelter, talk to the director, and ask if you can spend a day working with and talking to the people there. A number of possible experiences could be pursued. But what is important, no matter what tack taken, is that you try to get to know and understand some

of the individuals served by the shelter, to know and understand them as
human beings on their own terms. You can make this a formal or informal
endeavor. You could volunteer to work at the shelter for three to four
evenings during a month. You could offer to help serve food. No matter
what task you choose take the time and make the effort to get to know one
or two individuals. Don't hesitate to tell them about yourself, your aspirations to become a teacher, and don't hesitate to ask them about their school
experiences.

Visit an English as a Second Language (ESL) Pull-Out Session.   During one of your in-school practicums ask a school representative if you can
visit and observe a pull-out class instruction in ESL. During some of the
time sit and observe the students, the mode of instruction, and the interactions between teacher and students and among students. Consider examining some of the following questions: What is the focus of the lesson? Are
you acquainted with any of the students in the class and do you notice these
students interacting differently with the teacher or other students? What
does the student gain and or miss by being pulled out of their other class?

Visit a Women's Halfway House.   Contact the director of a halfway
house and see if you can volunteer some of your time. While there get to
know one or two individuals (or families). Explain to them your desire to
be a teacher and inquire (with both adults and children) about their school
experiences. In what ways have schools and teachers been an important or
insignificant force in their lives? What kind of educational contributions
might help to reduce the real need for a halfway house?

Shadowing a Culturally Different Child.   After having been in a particular school or classroom for a period of time (1–2 months) take the time
to spend an entire day (or two half days) "shadowing" and observing a child
who is culturally distinct from the school or classroom norm. As you follow
this child, note his or her interactions with other children, his or her
classroom participation, and the child's behavior in different school settings. Once you have observed the child, write up your observation with the
idea of raising and pursuing further questions. What questions arose and in
what way do you think the factor of "cultural difference" affected what you
observed?

Visit a Bilingual Classroom.   Ask a school representative if you could
visit a bilingual classroom. After arranging the visit spend some time in the
classroom acting both as an observer and as tutor for individuals. Some

questions to consider include: How are distinct languages used in instruction? Do the majority of students represent one language group? What does the classroom look like? What curriculum materials are available in the classroom?

A Home Visit. Having established yourself in one classroom and gotten to know the students, ask the teacher if she or he would make a home visit with you. The goals and purposes for home visits are many and varied. If this is not a common practice in your school or classroom, suggest that the visit be guided by a need to get to know a particular student whose classroom instruction could be enhanced but who does not represent a particular challenge. If such visits are common, or at least part of the practice, ask the teacher if you can go along on one. Work with the teacher to know both the purposes of the visit and ways to interact in the family's setting. After the visit talk with the teacher to better understand and process the experience.

A Community Visit. Pick a particular community in your city or area that seems "foreign" or unknown to you. See if you can find someone who knows this area and who will act as a "guide." Over the period of a few weeks take some excursions to that part of the city and get to know its stores, its churches, and its parks or recreations areas. How is this setting different from what you are used to?

School District Visits. Check out Jonathan Kozol's (1991) claim that within some districts and between others, the resources and educational opportunities vary significantly. Attend school board meetings in two different districts and compare and contrast the agenda issues and discussions. Arrange for formal visits to two different (elementary, middle, or high) schools that represent two distinct socioeconomic classes. Take note of and compare bricks and mortar resources, educational materials, classroom environments, and teacher work spaces.

Curriculum Resources. Take a look at the school district's curricular objectives and goals and your local classroom's curriculum materials. To what degree is there an expressed and evident concern for including materials that underscore the contributions and the perspectives of people of color? Where do you see this? If you do not find these themes what do you find? How are working-class and people of color portrayed?

CONCLUSION

There are, of course, numerous other experiences to be had and fruitful ways of examining those experiences. We hope that as a result of a reflective examination of these and other experiences you will look both inward and outward, forever maintain a commitment to all students' learning, and attempt to understand the obstacles and the pathways to success. Good luck.

BIBLIOGRAPHY

The following list includes both works referred to in the text and additional articles and books that we thought might be beneficial. We have tried to keep the list manageable and short. Works marked with an * are those that are cited in this volume.

Alba, R. D. (1990). *Ethnic identity: The transformation of White America*. New Haven, CT: Yale University Press.

*Anyon, J. (1980). Social class and the hidden curriculum of work. *Journal of Education, 162*, 67–92.

Apple, M. (1993). Constructing the "other": Rightist reconstructions of common sense. In C. McCarthy & W. Crichlow (Eds.), *Race identity and representation in education*. New York: Routledge.

*Apple, M. (1993). *Official knowledge*. New York: Routledge.

Asante, M. K. (1991). The afrocentric idea in education. *The Journal of Negro Education, 60*, 170–180.

*Asante, M. K. (1991/1992). Afrocentric curriculum. *Educational Leadership, 49*(4), 28–31.

Asante, M. K., & Ravitch, D. (1991). Multiculturalism: An exchange. *The American Scholar, 60*(2), 267–275.

Atlas, J. (1990). *Battle of the books: The curriculum debate in America*. New York: Norton.

Banks, J. (1988). *Multiethnic education: Theory and practice*. Boston: Allyn & Bacon.

*Banks, J. (1991/1992). Multicultural education: For freedom's sake. *Educational Leadership*, 32–36.

Banks, J. (1993). The canon debate, knowledge construction, and multicultural education. *Educational Researcher, 22*(5), 4–14.

Banks, J., & Banks C. (Eds.). (1989). *Multicultural education: Issues and perspectives*. Needham Heights, MA: Allyn & Bacon.

*Bell, D. (1992). *Faces at the bottom of the well: The permanence of racism*. New York: Basic Books.

Bennett, W. (1987). *James Madison High School: A curriculum for American students.* Washington, DC: U.S. Department of Education.

Bennett, W. (1988). *Our children and our country.* New York: Simon & Schuster.

*Bennett, W. (1992). *The de-valuing of America.* New York: Summit Books.

Bilingual Education Office, California State Department of Education. (1986). *Beyond language: Social and cultural factors in schooling language minority students.* Los Angeles: Evaluation, Dissemination and Assessment Center, California State Department of Education.

*Bourdieu, P., & Passeron, J. (1977). *Reproduction in education, society, and culture.* London: Sage.

Commins, N. (1989). Language and affect: Bilingual students at home and at school. *Language Arts, 66*(1), 29–43.

Cummins, J. (1984). *Bilingualism and special education: Issues in assessment and pedagogy.* Clevedon, UK: Multilingual Matters.

Cummins, J. (1986). Empowering minority students: A framework for intervention. *Harvard Educational Review, 56,* 18–36.

Cummins, J. (1989). *Empowering minority students.* Sacramento: California Association for Bilingual Education.

Delgado-Gaitan, C. (1987). Parents' perceptions of school: Supportive environments for children. In H. Trueba (Ed.), *Success or failure? Learning and the language minority student.* Cambridge, MA: Newbury House.

Delpit, L. (1986). Skills and other dilemmas of a progressive Black educator. *Harvard Educational Review, 56*(4), 379–385.

Delpit, L. (1988). The silenced dialogue: Power and pedagogy in educating other people's children. *Harvard Educational Review, 58*(3), 280–298.

Delpit, L. (1995). *Other people's children.* New York: New Press.

Deyhle, D. (1987). Learning failure: Tests as gatekeepers and the culturally different child. In H. Trueba (Ed.), *Success or failure? Learning and the language minority student.* Cambridge, MA: Newbury House.

D'Souza, D. (1991). *Illiberal education: The politics of race and sex on campus.* New York: The Free Press.

*Dewey, J. (1956). *The child and the curriculum/the school and society.* Chicago: The University of Chicago Press. (Original work published 1902)

*Duckworth, E. (1987). *The having of wonderful ideas and other essays on teaching and learning.* New York: Teachers College Press.

Finn, C. (1990). Narcissus goes to school. *Commentary, 89*(6), 40–45.

*Finn, C. (1991). *We must take charge.* New York: The Free Press.

Fordham, S., & Ogbu, J. (1986). Black students' school success: Coping with the burden of "acting White." *The Urban Review, 18,* 176–206.

Gates, H. L. (1992). *Loose cannons: Notes on the culture wars.* New York: Oxford University Press.

Gay, G. (1977). Curriculum design for multicultural education. In *Multicultural education: Commitments, issues and applications.* Washington, DC: Association for Supervision and Curriculum Development.

*Goodlad, J. (1984). *A place called school.* New York: McGraw-Hill.

Grant, C., & Sleeter, C. (1986). Race, class, and gender: An argument for integrative analysis. *Review of Educational Research, 56,* 195–211.

Grant, C., & Sleeter, C. (1989). *Turning on learning: Five approaches for multicultural teaching.* Columbus, OH: Merril.

Hale-Benson, J. (1982). *Black children: Their roots, culture and learning styles.* Baltimore, MD: Johns Hopkins University Press.

*Hacker, A. (1992). *Two nations: Black and White, separate, hostile, unequal.* New York: Ballantine.

*Heath, S. B. (1982). Questioning at home and at school: A comparative study. In G. Spindler & L. Spindler (Eds.), *Doing the ethnography of schooling: Educational anthropology in action.* New York: Holt, Rinehart & Winston.

*Heath, S. B. (1983). *Ways with words.* New York: Cambridge University Press.

*Hirsch, E. D. (1988). *Cultural literacy.* New York: Vintage Books.

hooks, b. (1990). *Yearning: race, gender, and cultural politics.* Toronto: Between the Lines.

*hooks, b. (1994). *Outlaw culture: Resisting representations.* New York: Routledge.

hooks, b., & West, C. (1991). *Breaking bread: Insurgent Black intellectual life.* Boston: South End Press.

*Kozol, J. (1991). *Savage inequalities.* New York: Crown.

*Kramer, R. (1991). *Ed school follies.* New York: The Free Press.

*Leonard, J. (1993). Listen to the dispossessed. *The Nation, 256*(4), 124.

*Lightfoot, S. L. (1978). *Worlds apart.* New York: Basic Books.

MacCann, D., & Woodward, G. (1977). *Cultural conformity in books for children.* Metuchen, NJ: The Scarecrow Press.

*Martin, J. R. (1992). *Schoolhome.* Cambridge, MA: Harvard University Press.

McCarthy, C. (1990). *Race and curriculum.* Bristol, PA: Falmer Press.

McCarthy C., & Crichlow, W. (Eds.). (1993). *Race identity and representation in education.* New York: Routledge.

*McIntosh, P. (1988). White privilege and male privilege: A personal account of coming to see correspondences through working in women's studies. (Working Paper No. 189). Wellesley, MA: Wellesley College, Center for Research on Women.

*McNeil, L. (1986). *Contradictions of control.* New York: Routledge & Kegan Paul.

*Meier, D. (1995). *The power of their ideas.* Boston: Beacon Press.

Moll, L. (1988). Some key issues in teaching Latino students. *Language Arts, 65*(5), 465–472.

Nieto, S. (1992). *Affirming diversity.* New York: Longman.

*Noddings, N. (1992). *The challenge to care in schools.* New York: Teachers College Press.

Oakes, J. (1985). *Keeping track: How schools structure inequality.* New Haven, CT: Yale University Press.

*Paley, V. (1989). *White teacher.* Cambridge, MA: Harvard University Press.

Perrone, V. (1989). *Working papers: Reflections on teachers, schools and communities.* New York: Teachers College Press.

*Ravitch, D. (1991). Multiculturalism: E Pluribus Plures. *The American Scholar, 59*(3), 337–56.

Ravitch, D., & Finn, C. (1987). *What do our 17-year-olds know?* New York: Harper & Row.

*Rodriguez, R. (1982). *Hunger of memory: The education of Richard Rodriguez.* Boston: David R. Godine.

Schlesinger, A. (1992). *The disuniting of America.* New York: Norton.

*Sizer, T. (1992). *Horace's school.* New York: Houghton Mifflin.

Sleeter, S. (Ed.). (1991). *Empowerment through multicultural education.* Albany, NY: SUNY Press.

Steele, S. (1990). *The content of our character.* New York: St. Martin's Press.

*West, C. (1993). *Race matters.* Boston: Beacon Press.

Zeichner, K. M., & Liston, D. P. (1996). *Reflective teaching: An introduction.* Mahwah, NJ: Lawrence Erlbaum Associates.

INDEX